Female Leadership

Navigate the minefield of modern life to become a fearless & confident leader.

Sophie Lawrence

Copyright © Sophie Lawrence Publishing

All rights reserved.
No part of this publication may be reproduced, distributed, or transmitted in any form or by any means, including photocopying, recording, or other electronic or mechanical methods, without the prior written permission of the publisher, except in the case of brief quotations embodied in critical reviews and certain other non-commercial uses permitted by copyright law.

Table of Contents

It's A New World 9

Chapter 1 – The Key to Modern Female Leadership 11

Lewin's Leadership Styles 13

Newer Leadership Styles and Models 15

Vital Lessons from the Past 18

The Differences in Recognized Female Leadership Roles 25

Chapter 2 – A Lack of Quality Female Leaders? 30

Differences Between Genders in Leadership 38

Do Enough Women Want To Be Leaders? 43

Chapter 3 – The Complicated 2nd Generation Gender Issues 49

Family and The Workplace 50

Unconscious Gender Bias and How To Get Around It 53

Real Life Case Study – Heather 64

Chapter 4 – Gender, Equality and Getting Your Worth 67

Questioning Femininity 72

Overcoming Social Constructs and Constraints 78

Chapter 5 – Breaking Gender Barriers Down Fast 80

The Vital Moves 89

Real Life Case Study – David 91

Chapter 6 – Your Own Choices 94

Achieving Confidence and Assertiveness 94

Ditch Perfectionism and Trying To 'Have It All' 99

Building Your Tribe 102

Chapter 7 – Broader Strategies For Everyday Use 112

The Case We Must Make 112

Real Life Case Study – How IBM Encourages Gender Diversity 119

Chapter 8 – The Rise and Rise of the Female Entrepreneur 122

How Women Are Leveraging Their Strengths In Entrepreneurial Endeavors 122

Female Entrepreneurs Work Differently 123

High Profile Women Entrepreneurs & The Lessons We Can Take 124

Industries That Fit Well with Feminine Skills 128

Building an Effective Online Business 130

Overcoming the Challenges of Starting your own Business 132

Chapter 9 – Nurturing The Next Generation Of Female Leaders 135

Combatting Gender Bias Fast 135

Real Life Case Study of Mentorship and Support 139

Conclusion: Be Strong, Lead, Find Success 141

Confidence & Assertive Skills for Women. 145

Introduction: Have The Confidence To Be A Strong, Calm Woman in the Modern World 146

It's Time For Massive Positive Change 149

Sample Stories 150

Consequences 152

Chapter 1 – Defining Terms For The Future 154

Real Life Case Study – Rebecca 154

Imposter Syndrome 155

Consequences Of The Confidence Gap 158

The Statistics 159

Are You Your Own Worst Enemy? 161

What Do We Mean By Assertiveness? 164

Real Life Case Study – Trinity 164

What Does Real Assertiveness Look Like? 166

Women's' Context Conscious Problem 167

Chapter 2 – Get Inspired to Make Changes 171

How Does Assertiveness Help You To Become More Self-Confident? 172

How To Have Less Stress and Have Stronger Relationships 173

Other Benefits of Being Assertive 177

Assertiveness in the Workplace 180

Chapter 3 – Assess Your Default Communication Style 185

The Assertive Style – the Holy Grail of Good Communication 188

The Aggressive Style – Bulldozing your Way Through Life 189

The Submissive Style – Head Down, Avoiding Conflict 192

The Passive-Aggressive Style – 'Cut Off Your Nose to Spite Your Face' 194

Who Dares Wins? 195

Is your Communication Style Hurting Your Career? 196

Chapter 4 – Confidence & Assertiveness: The Truth 201

The Solution 212

Flipping It 216

The Barriers to Destroy! 218

Part 2 – Strategies To Build Confidence 220

Confidence = Assertiveness = Success 220

Chapter 5 – Start With The Mind: Developing A Positive Mindset 222

Recognizing Negative Thinking 223

Turn that Frown Upside Down – Create a Positive Mindset 224

Real Life Case Study – Maria 227

Developing Mental Toughness 229

Chapter 6 – Play To Your Strengths 233

Emotional Intelligence 233

How To Quickly and Easily Improve Your Emotional Intelligence 236

Women's Intuition: Is It Real? 239

Chapter 7 – Faking It 'til You Make It 243

How to Appear Confident 243

The Body Language of a Confident, Assertive Person 245

Real Life Case Study – Jane 247

How Posture Influences Self-Confidence, Mood and Neurochemistry 250

Grin and Bear It: Reduce Stress Fast 251

Chapter 8 – Taking Risks, Seeking Courage, Finding Confidence 255

Behaviors to Build Courage Fast 256

Assertiveness in Context & Environment 264

Chapter 9 – Assertiveness in the Workplace 265

Real Life Case Study – Emma 270

Techniques For Being An Assertive Boss 271

When and How To Be Assertive with Anyone 272

How To Be An Assertive Employee At Work 273

Keeping Safe: Dealing With Sexual Harassment At Work 276

Assertiveness in Interviews 280

Example Scenarios and Assertive Responses 283

Real Life Case Study – Rachel 283

Chapter 10 – Assertiveness Closer to Home 285

Assertiveness With Loved Ones 285

Mindful Assertiveness 287

Appropriate Assertive Family Communication 291

Adopting Assertiveness In Difficult Everyday Situations 294

Real Life Case Study – Martine 298

Chapter 11 – Strong Communication for Strong Women... 307

Conclusion – How Assertive Women Can Change The World 312

The Power of Language 313

It's A New World

The fact that there are currently fewer female leaders than there are male ones is universally accepted. It's a situation that is slowly but surely changing, yet there's still a long way to go before the glass ceiling is shattered. Overt gender discrimination is becoming fairly rare, but discrimination nevertheless does still exists.

When you look at North American Fortune 500 companies, only around 6% of them are led by women. Yet 47% of the US working population are women, so why the enormous disparity?
Luckily though, things have been shifting for a long time in favor of a more equal gender balance for female leadership roles within workplaces.

Women are no longer content to sit back and accept unequal status, and there are hundreds of successful female leaders and entrepreneurs paving the way. If you're a woman who aspires to lead or to pursue entrepreneurship, then there's never been a better time to start.

If you're a business looking to increase the gender balance of leaders in your organization, then this book will explain why increasing the number of female leaders can bring more success and profitability. We'll also look at how you can encourage changes to allow more women opportunities to perform in top positions.

Leadership is about ability, not gender, but many inherent feminine traits lend themselves particularly well to leadership. In this book, we'll also explore how women can capitalize on their inherent feminine abilities to improve their leadership potential. We'll go against advising women to embrace more masculine qualities, that may not come naturally, and instead will seek to challenge the view that great leadership requires more than the traditionally viewed masculine traits. Instead, we'll explore the value of more feminine leadership styles and champion their use by women. We'll investigate the barriers you many come up against and explore how you can best overcome them.

In this book, we'll also investigate how employing and nurturing more female leaders can help businesses grow. There are numerous studies that show how women leaders are intrinsic to success. Having a blend of management styles across a business can make your business stronger in the long run. Over the course of the next nine chapters, we'll explore in further detail exactly what women bring to the table, and why we are so damn valuable.

Chapter 1 – The Key to Modern Female Leadership

"It's about knowing yourself and what you're good at. Females, males – anyone can be anything they want to be."
Payal Kadakia, Founder & Executive Chairman of ClassPass

Leadership In Context
For just one small word, leadership encompasses numerous ideas and values. The dictionary definition is the action of leading a group of people or an organization. However, real leadership goes way beyond that simple definition. And often what it means to lead is open to individual interpretation.

In a business context, leadership is how well senior managers in the organization set challenging goals, and inspire and motivate their people to achieve those goals. It's the way they drive the performance of the business to the highest levels possible. It's also how the management teams embody the company's vision and values, and how they motivate and inspire their employees to embody them.

When a business performs well, hits targets, and is level with or ahead of its competitors, this is down to good leadership. Poor performance correspondingly is usually a result of poor leadership. This is why you'll often see a change in leadership shortly after a business announces poor performance figures. Leadership sets the direction a company is headed in and then steers it towards that direction.

Awesome Female Leadership

Meg Whitman joined eBay in 1998 as CEO. At that time the company employed a total of 30 people and grossed $4,000,000 a year. By the end of 2008, under Whitman's leadership, the company had grown beyond all expectations. eBay now employed 15,000 people and grossed $8,000,000,000. She stepped down as CEO in 2008, but her legacy as an incredibly effective leader is indisputable. 2008 was also the year that she was inducted into the U.S. Business Hall of Fame.

So, what was it about Meg Whitman's leadership that brought eBay from a quirky, mildly successful business to a multi-billion dollar powerhouse?

Whitman gave the business some much-needed direction through her leadership.

She was passionate about putting customers first and transforming eBay's website from 'clunky' and difficult to use, to slick and user-friendly. She reorganized the company, splitting it into twenty-three different business categories and appointing executives to lead each category.

She was determined to set a clear vision and to make sure that everyone in the company understood the vision as well as their part to play in achieving it. She knew that for eBay to reach the success she envisioned, she'd need to have everybody on board.

To do this, Whitman also focused on employee engagement, believing that the best results come from a motivated and happy workforce. Her employees have been known to describe her as *'relentlessly optimistic'* and how they admired her ability to stay focused and positive.

As a result of Whitman's leadership style, employees were more empowered, the business functioned more efficiently, and customer satisfaction increased dramatically. Not to mention, of course, the profits!

Leadership Styles
All business leaders are mostly aiming for the same outcome – high profit and a stable business that can withstand unpredictable outside forces. However, the way they approach it can differ significantly.

There are numerous leadership styles and various models that explore the different ways people approach leadership. It would take an entirely new book to cover them all. So, for the purposes of this chapter, we'll look at a couple of the most common and influential leadership style models.

Lewin's Leadership Styles

One of the earliest studies into leadership styles was led by psychologist Kurt Lewin in 1939. Lewin and his team identified three core leadership styles, that formed a basis for later, more complex leadership theories.

The study involved assigning three groups of schoolchildren to be led by one of the three types of leader: democratic, autocratic, or laissez-faire. The researchers then noted the children's response and performance under the different types of leadership.

These three types of leadership are a common model used in leadership and management courses across the globe. Let's take a closer look at how the three different styles compare:

Autocratic Leadership
Autocratic leaders are authoritarian. They set clear expectations and timelines. Autocratic leadership sets a clear divide between the leader and the followers. In this leadership style, the leader makes all decisions independently, without seeking any input from their followers.

The positives of this style are that employees are given clear instruction and understand what is expected of them. It's useful in situations where deviation from rules and standards can have dramatic consequences. For example, it may be the style of leadership most appropriate to a heavily regulated industry.

The negatives are that it discourages creative thinking, it breeds poor employee engagement, and it can be seen as a very dictatorial style. It can create a very hostile environment when used inappropriately. Also, it can lead to an 'us and them' mentality where employees and leaders appear to be on opposite sides.

Autocratic leadership is generally considered quite an old-fashioned style of leadership that has more limitations than positives. It's a helpful style to adopt in certain situations that need a strong leader to take charge and make decisions, but it's rarely an appropriate style to use every day.

Democratic Leadership
Democratic leaders encourage group participation in activities and two-way discussion. They will often provide guidance and advice but are less likely to provide rigid

rules and instructions. They generally value the outcome over the process. Democratic leaders encourage followers to voice their opinions on decisions, but they retain the final say.

By encouraging participation, democratic leaders foster better engagement and more motivated followers. It also allows for more creative thinking and more effective teamwork.

In Lewin's study, this was considered to be the most effective leadership style. Although the children in this group produced less than the children in the Autocratic group, the output was of higher quality.

Laissez-Faire Leadership
Laissez-faire leaders provide very little direction or guidance and encourage followers to make decisions themselves with little or no input from the leader.

In Lewin's study, this group produced the least and had the most trouble both cooperating and working independently. They were also the most demanding of the leader.

Newer Leadership Styles and Models

Those three leadership styles are fairly polarizing, and few leaders fit neatly into those categories all of the time. However, Lewin's work provided a foundation for other studies into leadership theory that has expanded and developed into a variety of leadership styles.

Here are some of the more popular leadership styles that

have been identified.

Transactional Leadership
Transactional leadership is most closely related to Lewin's autocratic leadership style. In this leadership style, the relationship between leader and follower is completely transactional and usually based on financial compensation for tasks completed.

The transactional leader gives clear instructions and sets expectations. Followers are clear on what is expected of them, and what the expected compensation will be. Transactional leaders may offer incentives for high performance as a motivational tool, but they don't tend to recognize employee engagement as necessary or relevant to their organization.

Like autocratic leadership, this leadership style tends to result in less creative thinking. It's a suitable style for leaders in positions where their employees are producing high volumes like in manufacturing, or in high volume sales. It's least suitable for leaders who need their employees to solve complex problems or come up with creative solutions regularly.

Situational Leadership
Situational leadership is a leadership model that encompasses different styles. The basis of this model is that while there are different styles, they should vary by situation and not by the individual. It recognizes that different leadership challenges need different leadership approaches.

One of the most popular models of situational leadership is the *Hersey-Blanchard Model* that identifies four core leadership styles:

Telling – Much like the autocratic style, this is where the leader gives directions and expects them to follow without much question.

Selling – This is where the leader recognizes the need to persuade employees or followers to buy into an idea or vision.

Participating – This is where the leader encourages employees or followers to have an active role in decision making, but the leader remains hands-on and involved.

Delegating – This is like the laissez-faire style, where a leader steps back and allows the group a lot of autonomy over decisions.

The key to this model is that none of these styles are considered superior. They are all better suited to different situations, and a good leader will be able to identify and employ the appropriate style for any given situation.

In this model, the style a leader chooses will depend in part on the 'maturity' level of the employees, along with the task itself. Their 'maturity' level is their knowledge and competence in the role. For employees with low knowledge and competence, a delegating style would be inappropriate for most tasks, as those employees would need a high level of guidance and supervision. For highly skilled and competent employees, one of the more hands-off approaches would be suitable in most cases.

Transformational Leadership
Transformational leadership is a leadership style that is generally considered to be one of the most effective. Transformational leaders are excellent at motivating and

inspiring followers to achieve goals. They are usually energetic and passionate speakers, with high emotional intelligence. They value the individual contributions of their followers and readily offer praise and recognition.

Transformational leaders often take on a coaching and mentoring role with their employees. They look to support and develop the people they lead, nurturing their talents, and placing people in positions that suit their unique strengths.

This style is particularly well-suited to identifying how an organization needs to change and leading them through that change. Considering the fast pace of most industries in this day and age, the ability to lead change effectively is an essential skill for anyone aspiring to a leadership role.

In several studies, this style of leadership has been shown to drive higher staff engagement and higher performance than other styles. Meg Whitman is one example of a leader who embodied a transformational leadership style. In fact, studies have shown that women naturally tend to have a transformational leadership style. Leadership researcher Bernard Bass conducted one of the studies which concluded that women tend to have more characteristics aligned with transformational leadership.

Leadership theory is a thriving subject, and these leadership styles barely scratch the surface of the complex study of leadership. They do, however, provide a good basis for understanding some of the more common styles of leadership.

Vital Lessons from the Past

Although female leadership on the scale we know it today

is fairly new, there have been examples of women in leadership positions all throughout history. Women have led nations, founded religious organizations, built businesses and led social movements. And for most of history, they have done so against incredible odds.

Let's take a look at some of the most notable examples of historical women in leadership.

Cleopatra
Cleopatra is arguably one of the most famous women leaders of all time. Her infamous affairs with Roman leaders Julius Caesar and then later Mark Anthony sometimes overshadow her achievements as the last Pharaoh of Ptolemaic Egypt.

Her father was King Ptolemy XII. After his death, the throne passed to Cleopatra and her ten-year-old brother Ptolemy XIII. Cleopatra was 18 at the time. During this time, Egypt suffered from a poor economy and political turmoil.

Shortly after they ascended the throne, a rift began to appear between Cleopatra and her brother. The differences between them led to Cleopatra fleeing to Syria in order to assemble an army to take back the throne.

Eventually, it was a romantic alliance with Julius Caesar that saw Ptolemy XIII defeated and Cleopatra restored to the throne as Queen. After Caesar's death, Cleopatra was summoned to Rome by Mark Anthony, beginning her second affair with a Roman politician. Cleopatra ruled Egypt for around two decades, but there are few records of her achievements as a ruler. Most historical accounts concentrate on her influence over Roman politicians and not her own country.

It's said that Mark Antony killed himself after being defeated by his rival Octavian, and believing Cleopatra to be dead. When Cleopatra discovered this, she is said to have committed suicide by being bitten by an asp. The location of her burial has never been discovered.

Catherine The Great
Catherine II of Russia, also known as Catherine the Great, was Empress of Russia from 1762 until her death in 1796, and was the country's longest-ruling female leader. She gained the throne following a coup d'état against her unpopular husband Peter III. Catherine herself orchestrated the coup and seized the throne.

Catherine presided over a time of growth and stability for Russia. She modernized Russia, introduced inoculations and established the Smolny Institute for Noble Maidens – the first state-funded higher education institution for girls. She also pushed back against the power the church held within the state and encouraged the development of the economy.

Catherine had a great interest in education and culture. She was a patron of the arts and presided over the Russian Enlightenment. Her rule is often referred to as the Golden Age of Russia.

Queen Elizabeth I
Queen Elizabeth was the daughter of Henry VIII and Anne Boleyn. She ascended to the English throne in 1558, aged 25 after the death of her brother Edward VI.

She remained on the throne until her death in 1603, and reigned over a period of great change and growth. She introduced the first form of welfare in England and famously defeated the Spanish Armada. Elizabeth was also responsible for building on her father's legacy and transforming England into a country of Protestant faith. Her tolerant approach that allowed Puritans and Catholics to continue following their faith earned her a lot of approval. She still faced threats from Catholics however, who wanted to see her Catholic cousin Mary on the throne.

Elizabeth was an intelligent queen with a lot of political savvy. However, she was not without her critics. During her reign, Parliament became more influential, and there was conflict over several issues likes religion, her refusal to marry, and trade monopolies.

Elizabeth's reign is seen as a 'golden age' of English culture when Shakespeare was writing his plays and theatre became popular.

Queen Victoria
Another English Queen, Victoria reigned for 63 years and survived six potential assassination attempts. She was the first Queen to rule from Buckingham Palace and was the longest-serving British monarch until the reign of Elizbeth II. Victoria was Queen during the rapid expansion of the British Empire, and she eventually ruled over the largest empire in history.

She was, for the most part, a Queen who promoted peace and tolerance. Under her rule, all British colonies abolished slavery.

She married her first cousin, Prince Albert in 1840. Initially, Victoria ensured that Albert had no part in governing the country, but over time as she bore nine children, she relented and allowed him a larger political role.

To quell the growing republican movement, Victoria ushered in a new era of a more visible monarchy. She became a patron of numerous charities and made hundreds of civic visits. After Albert's death, however, she withdrew from public life and spent the majority of her time at Balmoral.

She did reemerge into the public eye later, and her Golden and Diamond Jubilees were widely celebrated across the British Empire.

Anna Bissell
When Anna Bissell's husband died in 1889, Anna became the very first female CEO in the United States. She was by all accounts a very effective leader, bringing the Bissell brand of carpet cleaners and vacuums to the international market.

Under her leadership, the company went from strength to strength and reportedly even Queen Victoria insisted on there being a Bissell at Buckingham Palace. By 1899 Bissell was the largest organization of its kind.

Anna Bissell was the embodiment of a transformational leader, implementing labor policies like pension plans before these were the norm.

Eleanor Roosevelt
Eleanor Roosevelt was the first First Lady to take an active political role. Up until President Roosevelt's election, the function of a First Lady was purely social. However, Eleanor had been campaigning on her husband's behalf throughout his political career. She'd also established businesses of her own in a factory to help Hyde Park families supplement their income, and bought and taught in

a girls school.

When her husband was elected, Eleanor was not content to sit back and attend social functions. Instead, she paved the way for future First Ladies by holding press conferences, writing a newspaper column, and supporting civil rights movements, among other activities.

Even after her husband's death, Eleanor continued to have political influence. She campaigned for presidents including John F Kennedy, was appointed as a United Nations delegate, and continued to support civil rights movements.

Indira Gandhi
Indira Gandhi was the first (and, at the time of writing, the only) female Prime Minister of India. She is also the second-longest serving Prime Minister. Gandhi served for several terms but was assassinated by her own bodyguards in October 1984.

Gandhi's introduction to politics began when she served as her father's personal assistant during his own time as Prime Minister. During this time, she was elected as President of the Indian National Congress. After her father's death, she joined the cabinet as Minister of Information and Broadcasting. In 1966 she was elected as Prime Minister of India.

Gandhi took India to war with Pakistan in 1971, and under her leadership, India's armed forces were victorious. That victory led to the creation of Bangladesh, and Gandhi was the first government leader to recognize the new country.

After a challenge from the opposition party that could have seen her banned from politics for six years, Gandhi appealed to the Supreme Courts. When their response was not what she anticipated, she declared a state of emergency throughout India. During this time she assumed emergency powers, imprisoned her opponents and passed several new laws. Many of her measures were highly unpopular and included a mass sterilization drive.

Emergency rule ended in 1977, and along with it, Gandhi's tenure as Prime Minister. In 1980, however, she was re-elected as Prime Minister once more and served until her assassination. Her final term was once again filled with controversy, predominantly over the handling of escalating conflict with Sikh separatists.

Barbara Jordan
Barbara Jordan was both the first woman and the first African-American to deliver a keynote speech at a Democratic National Convention.

Jordan studied political science and history at college, and then went on to graduate law school and passed the bar in 1960. She was inspired to become an attorney in high school after hearing a speech delivered by Edith S. Sampson.

Jordan opened a private law practice in 1960 and later won a seat in the Texas Senate in 1966. She was re-elected to the Texas Senate in 1968 and served until 1972, when she was elected to the House of Representatives. She was the first women elected in her own right to represent Texas in the House.

Perhaps Jordan's most memorable moment was delivering a speech before the U.S. House Judiciary Committee, supporting the impeachment of President Richard Nixon. Her eloquent and intelligent speech is often credited as the reason that Nixon resigned, recognizing that he could not defend the points that Jordan eloquently raised.

Margaret Thatcher
Margaret Thatcher was the first female Prime Minister of the United Kingdom. She was also the longest-serving British Prime Minister of the 20th-century. Thatcher held office for three full terms from 1979 until 1990. She was renowned for her uncompromising leadership style and was commonly known in the press as the 'Iron Lady'.

Thatcher was always a controversial figure in British politics, mostly due to her hardline policies and her drive to privatize national services. Her popularity nosedived during a period of recession and high unemployment, and her financial and anti-unionist policies were frequently met with resistance from the opposition

One of her most controversial actions was the closure of a number of British mines, and her refusal to meet the demands of the miner's union. A year-long miners' strike ensued, and eventually, the union conceded.

During the 1980s, Thatcher was often described as the most powerful woman in the world. In 1999, Time Magazine listed her as one of the most important people of the 20th century.

The Differences in Recognized Female Leadership Roles

While history provides a rich source of evidence that women can successfully lead, female leadership hasn't been taken seriously until more recently. One of the reasons for that is very few women rose to a leadership position in their own right. Most historical female leaders obtained their position from either privilege of birth or privilege of marriage. Often their leadership was controversial in some way, and all the more complicated for them being female.

Cleopatra had a valid claim to the Egyptian throne, but it took an alliance and an affair with a powerful man to secure her position. When the throne was secured, she was, by most non-Western accounts around that time, a great ruler and a keen scholar and scientist. Unfortunately, her actual achievements as a leader are glossed over in historical accounts with her affairs taking center stage over her leadership skills.

For the vast majority of women throughout history, the idea of them being able to hold the kind of positions that were open to men was unthinkable.

Of course, some of the historical barriers to leadership have always been class and not just purely gender. However, the fact remains that even women born to wealthy households for most of history would not have been encouraged to aspire to much beyond becoming a dutiful wife and good mother.

In the list above, Margaret Thatcher stands out as one woman who carved out a highly successful political career on the back of her own achievements. However, it's interesting to note that her leadership style is often described in more masculine terms. More often than not this is in a detrimental tone rather than celebratory of her strengths. She was certainly more of an autocratic leader than a laissez-faire one. It could also be argued that at times she demonstrated traits consistent with a transformational leader, for example, having the vision and ability to pull an entire country through a period of significant change. Factually, she left Britain financially stronger than she found it, regardless of people's opinions on how she achieved that. Something that is not often recognized and celebrated.

The Glass Ceiling

As just explored, historically, there were female leaders but they were the outliers, anomalies and they often faced severe opposition. In the early 20th century, women were still not allowed to vote. And even after gaining the vote in 1920 and getting a boost on the path to equality, leadership positions remained out of reach due to a lack of equal education opportunities.

Women were still denied access to many higher education opportunities, including Ivy League colleges. Getting a degree from a college like Harvard was impossible until 1963. And without access to those opportunities, women were poorly placed to step into leadership positions.

Fortunately, present-day situations are changing, albeit too slowly. A small number, 6% of leaders in Fortune 500 companies are now women but until 1972, when Katherine Graham became CEO of the Washington Post, there were none at all. So, when did thinking start to shift from leadership being a male-only occupation to it being possible for women to be considered?

A lot of this shift in mentality has only happened over the last 100 years.

Even with a good college education, women were only expected to fulfill secretarial and admin roles. Few, if any, corporations would even consider interviewing a woman for a management position or a professional role. The reasoning for this inequality was accepted social gender roles – men should be the breadwinners and women should be looking after the home and children.

It wasn't until the 1970s that these views were challenged and began to shift slightly. The Equal Rights movements influence meant women were no longer explicitly excluded from managerial roles and all professional occupations. However, there were still limits on what they could achieve. Only lower levels of management were attainable, yet, it was a move in the right direction.

The oft-used term 'glass ceiling' to describe the invisible but very real barrier preventing women from accessing higher-level leadership roles, was first used by the Wall Street Journal in 1986.

The concept of the glass ceiling caught on quickly, and eventually US Congress established an investigatory commission specifically for the 'Glass Ceiling' idea. In their report, they noted that the glass ceiling was driven by the notion that women were likely to quit working to start a family. No executives were willing to hire women for important roles because of the possibility that they might start a family.

New laws were passed to prevent the overt exclusion of women from leadership roles. And as a result, over a length of time, we've seen a rise in the number of female leaders in high-level positions. On a positive note for women in the present day, it's now easier than it's ever been for women to rise through the ranks of leadership. Unfortunately, the path to higher levels of leadership for women still isn't as clear as it is for their male counterparts but the situation is progressing at a rapid pace.

It's not true that women are better leaders than men, nor is it true that men are better leaders than women. Ability and talent are determined by many things, such as upbringing, socio-economic background, genetics, education, and environment – NOT GENDER!

However, it is true that men have always been given more opportunities to lead than women have. In the next chapter, we'll look at what, if any, general differences there are between men and women when it comes to leadership. We'll also explore why it is that there still a lack of female leaders in the 21st Century?

Chapter 2 – A Lack of Quality Female Leaders?

"A woman can and should be able to do any political job that a man can do."
Richard M. Nixon, 37th President of the United States.

Women's rights have come a very long way from women being both unable to vote and being unable to hold positions other than secretarial roles. Women serve in armies all over the world; they are business leaders, political leaders, and have the same legal status as any male in the USA.

So why then, are we seeing so few female leaders in the business and political arena? In this chapter, we'll take a look at some of the possible reasons that there's a general lack of female leaders.

Are Men Actually Better Leaders?

One of the reasons that women were initially excluded from leadership positions was the belief that women have a 'temperament' that makes them unsuitable to lead. Even President Nixon, despite the above quote, was heard saying 'off the record' that *"I don't think a woman should be in any government job whatever. I mean, I really don't. The reason why I do is mainly because they are erratic. And emotional. Men are erratic and emotional, too, but the point is a woman is more likely to be."* This coming from a man who was publicly supportive of women's rights makes this comment all the more insulting. It demonstrates how insidious barriers have historically prevented women from achieving their full potential.

As barriers were slowly but surely removed, women began to face a critical issue. To move past this invisible barrier they could either adopt stereotypically masculine behavior or accept that leadership would be out of their reach.

Unfortunately, even this 'solution' of adopting masculine behaviors came with its own set of problems. Women who behaved like men might have been more likely to be considered for leadership positions, but they'd still come under intense scrutiny and criticism for not acting like a woman. Add to this the fact that the behaviors that garner respect and admiration in men can generate distrust and cause a loss of respect when displayed by a woman.

This belief that women have trouble controlling their emotions persists to some extent to this day, although it's no longer such a widespread belief. Women's perceived intrinsic qualities are now more often seen as positive in leadership positions rather than a reason for them to be excluded.

According to 2018 research by Pew, most Americans agree that women are more skilled at encouraging and supporting, while men are considered better at decision-making and problem-solving. The numbers from the Pew research are very illuminating, and unless otherwise specified, it is this research that will be referred to in this chapter.

However, the invisible barriers are still there. Various studies have shown that men are generally taken more seriously at work. When a suggestion is made by a man it tends to be received more positively than if a suggestion is made by a woman. Even when the idea is presented in the same way, using the same language, the men are taken more seriously.

It's worrying that people have a different perception of the same behavior depending on which gender it comes from. When male leaders communicate unpopular decisions like job cuts, it's less likely to make them less popular with employees, who perceive them as effective leaders who make decisions in line with what's necessary for the business. On the other hand, when the same decisions are taken by female employers, they lose their popularity and receive strong criticism, as demonstrating qualities like strength and dominance is unfeminine behavior.

Women who demonstrate more stereotypically feminine behavior, like demonstrating compassion, are more popular but tend to be perceived as less competent. The more competent and strong they look to employees, the less popular they become. For female leaders, it's a catch-22 situation.

In a 1992 review of studies on gender and leadership, it was found that female leaders were usually evaluated as positively as male ones. There was, however, a difference between how women leaders with a more autocratic style were viewed in comparison to male leaders with the same style. The women were much less likely to be viewed positively than the men.

In a later 2008 study of gender differences in transformational and transactional leaders, research participants rated female transformational leaders more positively on extra effort, satisfaction, and effectiveness. In addition, female research participants rated female transformational leaders more positively.

Although there are still people who hold these outdated beliefs about how men are better leaders than women, the facts simply don't support this belief. For example, research by the Peterson Institute for International Economics revealed a correlation between higher profits and the number of women at the 'C-Suite'. Companies with more leadership positions filled by women, had at least 1% higher net profit margin when compared to companies without female leaders.
For example, Apple is one of the top-performing Fortune 500 companies, and it's no coincidence that they also have a comparatively high percentage of women leaders at 29%.

There's plenty of good news about how perspectives are shifting when it comes to gender differences in leadership. The Pew research confirms that the majority of Americans would like to see more women both in top corporate and top political leadership positions. The nationally representative survey of 4,587 adults was conducted online June 19-July 2, 2018.

According to the survey, most people do believe men still have an easier path to the top and that women have to do more to prove their worth. However, it does confirm that Americans largely see men and women as equally capable when it comes to the key qualities and behaviors that are essential for leadership. This even though the majority do believe that men and women in top leadership positions in business and politics do tend to have different leadership styles.

Out of those people who believe men and women have different approaches to leadership, 62% say neither approach is better. For those who feel one gender has a better approach, 22% say women's approach is best, 15% say men have a better approach.

For leadership in both business and politics, most respondents believe that men and women are equally strong in key leadership qualities, but where people see a difference, tends to be the women that they see as stronger in most areas. One key area where people believe women are better than men is in being compassionate and empathetic, and a large number believe women are better at working out compromises and standing up for what they believe in.

Although women have the edge in being seen to demonstrate compassion, this may not be seen as very helpful in their leadership career. 46% of Americans do view compassion as a positive trait for men in politics, however, only 29% say it mostly helps men in business. Instead, nearly half of the public (47%) says being compassionate makes no difference in helping a man get ahead, and 22% say it hurts men in the workplace. The results for women echo this sentiment.

Overall, male leaders are seen as better than female leaders in willingness to take risks and negotiating profitable deals. Compared to compassion and empathy, these are more recognizably useful traits in a leadership position.

When it comes to business leadership, in particular, women have a slight edge in creating a safe and respectful workplace and being honest and ethical. These are also two traits that Americans see as crucial to being a good business leader. For creating a safe and respectful workplace, 43% say women are better, 52% say there is no difference, and only 5% say men are better at this.

And while the majority of respondents say there is no difference between male and female leaders when it comes to valuing people from different backgrounds, considering the impact of business decisions on society, providing guidance and mentorship to young employees, and providing fair pay and good benefits, those who do see a difference tend to believe women are better at these competencies.

Women are much more likely than men to agree that female business leaders are better than their male counterparts at creating a safe and respectful workplace and providing mentorship to young employees. The majority believe that women and men are equally capable of handling key policy areas and running companies across industries.

On the whole, people are positive about the benefits of female leadership. 69% of respondents say that having more women in top positions in business and government would likely improve the quality of life for all Americans. 77% believe more women leaders would improve the quality of life for women specifically. When asked if more women leaders would improve the quality of life for men, 57% agreed it would.

Unsurprisingly, women are more likely than men to agree that more women in top leadership positions would be beneficial overall. Over 65% of women believe having more female leaders would improve the quality of life for men, compared with 47% of men.

When asked whether certain personal characteristics would help or hinder men and women seeking to succeed in business or politics, approximately 70% believed that being assertive and ambitious would help a man's chances in both business and politics. Around half of respondents see assertiveness and ambition as helpful to women who are aiming for top leadership positions. In comparison, about a quarter believe being assertive and ambitious can actually hurt a woman's chances of getting ahead in politics and business.

One attribute that's considered more helpful to women than to men is physical attractiveness. 60% of respondents believe it helps women get ahead in both politics and business.

Openly showing emotion was seen as being more harmful than helpful to both men and women. However, it was seen as more harmful for female leaders than male leaders. 52% say openly showing emotions hurts women in politics, but only 39% say this about men.

Some of these results echo the 2012 leadership research by Zenger and Folkman. More than 7,300 leaders were studied and scored against sixteen identified leadership competencies.

Women scored higher than men on twelve of these competencies, including:

- Takes initiative
- Practices self-development
- Displays high integrity and honesty
- Drives for results
- Develops others
- Inspires and motivates others
- Builds relationships
- Collaboration and teamwork
- Establishes stretch goals
- Champions change
- Solves problems and analyzes issues

- Communicates powerfully and prolifically

Men and women were rated equally in:

- Connects the group to the outside world
- Innovates
- Technical or professional expertise

The only area where men outscored women was in the ability to develop a strategic perspective. Even here, the researchers posited that more senior leaders always score higher on this competency. Because most top-level leaders are male, the aggregate scores favor men. However, when you compare only leaders at the top level, women and men are rated equally.

This survey is particularly interesting as it measured the perspective of leader's employees, peers, and managers. Instead of asking people if they thought women were better than men, they were rating an individual leader that they worked closely with, without overtly considering gender. Women consistently outperformed men in almost every single competency. Even more interesting is the fact that the higher the level of leadership, the more likely it was that women would score higher than their male counterparts.

The evidence is clear – men do not make naturally better leaders.

Unfortunately, despite the evidence to the contrary, even women tend to believe that men are better leaders. According to the Pew research, most women show a preference for male leaders. Even though studies like the Zenger Folkman research consistently demonstrate that male leaders are not more competent than their female colleagues, this leadership gender bias is demonstrated by both men and women.

Differences Between Genders in Leadership

Although men and women are both effective leaders, there are some general differences in typical leadership styles. It's important to stipulate here that not every male leader will be typical, nor every female leader. There are lots of leaders who naturally have a different leadership style than that is typical of their gender and it isn't necessarily because they feel the pressure to adapt their natural behavior.

With that said, here's a breakdown of the key differences that researchers have observed in leadership styles:

Male Leadership Style
Typically, men lean heavily towards a more transactional leadership style. They place a large emphasis on achieving goals. They tend to expect to provide direction and have that direction followed. Each task their employees complete is a transaction that is either successful or unsuccessful and depending on the outcome, employees should be either disciplined or rewarded.

They don't feel compelled to explain most of their decisions, as they don't believe that their employees need anything more than the transactional reward of salary and/or bonuses for motivation. They often take a hands-off approach to leading and keep themselves separate from their teams. This separation can be seen as a positive among employees, who are left to 'get on with it', however, it can become an issue if an employee needs support that the transactional leader is unwilling to provide.

Men value the clarity associated with a strong hierarchical structure and are more likely to enforce hierarchical boundaries. They consider these boundaries necessary to make sure that everyone is clear on their tasks and responsibilities.

Female Leadership Style

Typically, women lean more towards a transformational approach. They also emphasize on achieving key goals, but they take a more involved approach to achieve them. Female leaders are more hands-on with their teams and look for ways to motivate them beyond a transactional system of discipline and reward. They place more emphasis on their team's personal development and tend to provide explanations for their decisions. They are also more likely to consult their team's on decisions and take input from others – making decisions a more collaborative effort. Female leaders provide a higher level of support to their employees and they value teamwork and effective communication.

Transformational leaders have higher performance rates and more engaged employees. Their motivational style encourages creativity, teamwork, and communication. Detractors of the transformational style consider transformational leaders to be too 'soft' and reluctant to tackle poor performance. This, however, is not true. Transformational leaders do still implement disciplinary action where they find it appropriate, but they tend to take a 'will' vs 'skill' approach when deciding what action is appropriate. Poor performers that they believe simply need support to develop skill will be given support and encouragement. However, where employees are seen to be underperforming because of behavior rather than lack of

ransformational leaders will take disciplinary
es.

Transformational leadership is commonly seen among women leaders. One of the reasons that women are more likely to adopt a transformational leadership style is that it naturally lends itself to feminine traits like compassion and communication. As we've already noted, adopting a more masculine, autocratic approach can backfire for women. A transformational style allows them to leverage their gender's natural strengths.

Female leaders focus more on collaboration and the sharing of ideas across teams and departments. Female leaders are more likely to attribute credit for success to employees, without overemphasizing their own personal contribution. Conversely, when unsuccessful, they are less likely to blame others or put it down to bad luck. Instead, they are more likely to question their own competence.

Women are less likely to enforce hierarchical boundaries. Instead, they take a holistic approach to managing the team environment and pay more attention to ensure they treat every employee fairly.

What Drives The Differences In Leadership Styles Between Genders?

Numerous experts have pointed out that these differences begin in childhood, where societal gender expectations see more boys enrolled in sports teams and encouraged to engage in competitive behavior. Girls are encouraged more towards gentler and creative pursuits like dance.

These stereotypical expectations influence us right through to adulthood. In the workplace, males are more likely to view work as a competitive situation where there are winners and losers. Women are less likely to view work through the lens of being a competition.

These differences are slowly changing as more girls participate in team sports and gender expectations are less rigid. However, change is slow and we still place different expectations on males than we do on females.

While there are some noted differences in leadership style between the genders, it's this kind of intense focus on the differences that can serve to keep female leaders firmly below the glass ceiling.

Similarities Between Genders in Leadership
There are many more similarities between genders when it comes to how they lead than there are differences. So, let's take a look at how leaders are similar regardless of gender.

In many cases, it's the organizational culture that drives leadership behaviors more than gender. In a collaborative, non-hierarchical organization that emphasizes employee development, leaders are more likely to adopt transformational leadership behaviors. In a hierarchical, production-driven environment, behaviors consistent with transactional leadership will be adopted. Hiring managers look for leadership styles that fit with corporate culture, and so leaders that display a style congruent with the organization will stand a better chance of being hired.

In the Pew research, on the whole, the responses indicated that respondents didn't view many key leadership traits as significantly different for females or males. Competent leadership requires a blend of many different skills and competencies. Often, the specific competencies that a leader is strong in, are related to the context of the organization and are less dependent on gender.

One problem with perceived differences in leadership styles is that the terms used are subjective. People expect women to be more compassionate than men, and men to be more logical than women. This expectation can lead to them rating leaders differently based on gender expectations rather than reality. This can happen unconsciously, and so is potentially reflected in studies even when the questions are not overtly gender-specific.

Effective leadership requires several key competencies, none of which are exclusive to either gender. These competencies are skills that can be learned and developed by anybody regardless of gender.

Then there's the fact that the vast number of obvious and subtle differences between individual leaders goes way beyond gender differences. There are many compassionate and collaborative male leaders, just as there are many authoritarian and competitive female leaders.

Here's a list of the key traits that are commonly accepted as required for any individual to be an effective leader:

- Honesty and integrity
- Confidence
- Inspiring and motivating others
- Commitment and passion
- Good communication
- Decision making
- Problem-solving
- Delegation
- Innovation
- Empathy

As we've seen, women have the edge on some of these, but

none are exclusively female traits. Plenty of men are empathetic, and many women are very decisive. Being an effective leader is more about individually having the right blend of skills and capabilities to suit the job.

But if inherent gender traits aren't the reason that fewer women are in leadership positions, what's causing the disparity? One theory is that women simply don't want the responsibility of a high-level leadership position.

Do Enough Women Want To Be Leaders?

In 2003, an influential article was published in The New York Times. Journalist Lisa Belkin investigated why a growing number of successful women were 'opting out' of the corporate ladder, choosing to stay at home and raise their children instead.

The women featured had been afforded opportunities that women only twenty's five years earlier could only have dreamed of. They had Ivy League educations, prestigious law degrees and had gone on to gain prestigious positions in various organizations. The barriers to top-level leadership were coming down, and these women had the credentials to seize a piece of this power.

So why were they opting out of corporate life in high numbers? In the article, a theory was quoted that these women never broke through the glass ceiling because they were stopped by the 'maternal wall.' Those who didn't leave the world of work entirely were scaling down, reducing their hours and were not chasing higher positions in their organizations.

In the article, it noted that Fortune magazine had found that of the 108 women who had appeared on its list of the top 50 most powerful women, over 20 had since decided to leave their high-powered roles.

Why don't women rule the world? The article asks. Because they don't want to is the answer given.

Fast forward to the present day, and the idea of the opt-out revolution has come under a lot of scrutiny. In follow-up articles, many of the women had chosen to re-enter the world of work. They often took lower roles than those they'd occupied before, but many of them expressed some level of regret at giving up their ambition.

In 2013, a follow-up article was printed in the New York Times titled, *'The Opt-Out Generation Wants Back In.'* In the article, Judith Warner explored how the women featured in the original article and surrounding publicity now held different attitudes towards their decision to opt-out. In some cases, the women had since divorced and were left without the financial cushion of their husband's income that they'd relied upon to have the choice of opting out. For others, they felt that their identity and how their husbands viewed them had changed since opting out – and not for the better.

Another criticism leveled at the article has been that it focused on a very specific group of women. Predominantly white, middle class and privileged in terms of education, they were also married to affluent husbands and had the financial ability to choose to opt-out. For the majority of the female workforce 'opting out' has never really been a viable option.

So, is there an element of truth in the idea that women opt

themselves out of leadership roles once they marry and/or start a family?

The answer is complex. Yes, it's based on some truth. Women do often feel that they need to choose between career and family. There are still lingering societal pressures that make women feel like they are somehow failing their children if they aren't devoting their whole life to their upbringing. Combined with the fact that workplaces are generally more hostile places for working mothers, it feels easier for many women to either leave the workplace entirely or to accept that they will have to be content with lesser roles more 'suitable' for a working mother.

While more and more organizations have started to implement more family-friendly policies, it's still the case that flexibility simply isn't available in most workplaces. To 'get ahead' workers feel they need to work extra hours and spend as much time as possible in the office. Leaving early to spend time with their families or to take care of childcare responsibilities is often frowned upon in a lot of workplace cultures.

Requiring a degree of flexibility because of family responsibilities can be seen as being unreliable, and hiring managers can be put off by a woman who has children. Despite laws being put in place to discourage discrimination, it's easy for hiring managers to cite other reasons for rejection.

What this means is that while women might say they choose to stay home, the reality is that not all of them are making the choice freely. Often, giving up their ambitions is the only 'choice' they have.

Does Either Gender Really Make A More Effective Leader?

We've seen that in many competencies, women are considered more effective than men. The competencies where they are highest rated are those most commonly associated with transformational leadership. As leadership theory has evolved, transformational leadership is becoming the preferred style of leadership across most industries. Because of this, women do have a slight natural advantage.

Men, however also have natural characteristics that can lend themselves to a more transformational style. And like any other skill, these competencies can be learned.

The context of leadership is also relevant to how effective any individual leadership style is. The military, for example, lends itself to a more autocratic style. And the most effective leaders adapt their style for changing circumstances. While the inclusive nature of transformational leadership is an asset in many situations, a leader who won't make any decisions without consensus agreement is likely to lose trust and respect quite quickly. For urgent decisions that don't have a wide impact, a more autocratic decision-making process is much more effective.

The best leaders are those that understand the need for flexibility in leadership style regardless of gender or personal characteristics.

There's evidence to suggest that a more female-oriented style of leadership that takes a more mentoring and coaching style is best received in a more female-dominated environment. In a more male-dominated environment, a more autocratic and commanding style is better received.

In most modern organizations, a transformational leadership style is most effective. Large, successful businesses like Google and Apple are concentrating on removing rigidly hierarchical structures to promote creativity and problem-solving. The transformational, motivational style that emphasizes employee development and mentoring works very well in organizations like this.

In more hierarchical organizations like the military, this approach is less suitable. With clear and distinct boundaries and responsibilities between the different levels of leadership, a more autocratic approach ensures everyone understands their role. And when mistakes can have serious and far-reaching consequences, a transactional approach that rewards compliance and disciplines rule-breakers can be necessary.

Despite the already noted differences in male and female leadership styles, both men and women make effective leaders. The differences are apparent in various studies, but the percentages are small. The context of the leadership environment also has a large part to play.

It's also prudent to note that regardless of the study trends, psychologists have cautioned against concluding that either gender has a specific, natural management style. The research only demonstrates averages, and there is wild variance among individuals. It's also possible that women, having seen that adopting masculine behaviors has the undesired effect of making them unpopular, have consciously adapted towards more traditionally feminine traits.

Although the Fortune 500 is low on female CEOs, according to the Bureau of Labor Statistics, when you look at US organizations overall, nearly 25% of chief executives are women. On the surface, this looks like a big step forward, but these figures include small businesses with only a handful of employees.

Issues like the so-called Opt-Out Revolution are just the tip of the iceberg when it comes to reasons why there are significantly fewer female leaders. In Chapter Three, we'll investigate the second generation issues that could be holding women back from reaching their full leadership potential.

Chapter 3 – The Complicated 2nd Generation Gender Issues

"Women are not born, they are made."
Simone de Beauvoir, French writer, intellectual, existentialist philosopher, political activist, feminist and social theorist.

Gender Bias Issues

First-generation gender issues are the kind of issues we've briefly looked at so far. Open discrimination and exclusion from leadership or other positions were issues that our grandmothers and great-grandmothers often had to face. They were difficult to battle because they were deep-rooted, and society needed to change the way it viewed women in order to make a change. Overall, those big public battles have been won today.

There are federal laws in place protecting women from workplace discrimination. There are more women leaders than ever before, and society is constantly shifting towards a more positive view of women in high-powered roles.

Second-generation gender issues are less obvious and are more difficult to battle because so many people don't believe they exist or don't see them because of their subtlety. Many, but not all are workplace issues linked to policies created with male mindset or values. These are not intentional, and often seem to be completely non-sexist. However, they provide invisible barriers that prevent more women from rising through organizations to leadership roles.

In fact, second-generation issues are so subtle; many

women deny that they even exist. Yet research and studies have shown that they do, and they create very real barriers to women's success. For women experiencing these barriers, it can be very frustrating to be up against an almost invisible wall between you and workplace success.

So, what exactly are these barriers? How can you identify them? And how do you deal with them? In this chapter, we'll explore some of the most common second-generation issues in more detail.

Family and The Workplace

While men are contributing more to family responsibilities like childcare and housework than ever before, the simple fact is that women are usually still expected to be the main caregiver in the family.

When women choose to start a family, they are often diverting or delaying their career prospects, knowingly or not. Even with flexible working, family-friendly employer policies and a supportive husband, having children has a very real impact on women's careers.

Workplaces are usually not designed to support workers who may need flexibility in terms of hours and location. Many women are left with no alternative but to work part-time hours, which are usually lower-paid roles. Even if a woman manages to fulfill contracted hours in a full-time position, they are often barred from promotion by other invisible barriers.

Workplaces value employees who work longer hours, as it's seen to demonstrate commitment and ambition. Yet fulfilling contractual hours while also fulfilling caring duties and maintaining high-performance levels should also demonstrate the same thing. Unfortunately, as a society, we do not tend to see it this way or place value on such things.

Sometimes promotions may need extensive travel that would not be possible for a person who has family commitments. These requirements put women at a distinct disadvantage. Add this to the fact that if they have an ambitious spouse or partner, he will usually work long hours and do the traveling required – leaving the woman to pick up any additional family responsibilities. The idea that the woman would work the longer hours while the man makes career sacrifices more often than not isn't on the table for discussion.

What this means is that women 'choose' roles that are more flexible but have fewer, if any, opportunities for promotion.

If questioned about this, the usual response from hiring managers is 'but that's just what's needed for the job – regular travel, long hours, attending meetings.' Yet now, more than ever before, most things are possible to accomplish remotely. Live video calling and streaming mean that you can attend a meeting without setting foot in a meeting room and still get the benefits of face-to-face interaction with clients and colleagues.

There's another, insidious barrier affecting even women who choose not to have children – or find that they are not able to have children. Employers tend to discriminate against women who are of childbearing age, because of the expectation that at some point, the woman will have children. So where male colleagues are reaching the prime of their career, gaining promotions or successfully being hired by bigger and better organizations, women are struggling to be considered seriously because they pose the 'risk' to employers that they might have a child.

The impact of childcare responsibilities on women's careers is well-studied and accepted by most people. However, there's a hidden caring issue that impacts women more than men: taking care of elderly relatives.

When a parent or an in-law becomes unable to take care of themselves or needs extra support, it's usually the women of the family that provide that support. All too often, this happens just as the woman's childcare responsibilities are finished and her children are finally adults or older teenagers. As a result, many women who dreamed of picking up their careers once the children had grown up are faced with yet another dilemma: be there for someone they love that needs them, or put their career first. Understandably, it's their career that usually suffers.

While federal legislation does exist that provides some level of protection for pregnant women, the level of protection for women with childcare responsibilities varies by state. And there is nothing in place to protect people who care for elderly or disabled relatives.

Regardless of the reason behind women's roles as default caregivers, these extra responsibilities place a burden on their careers. Workplaces that don't have appropriately family-friendly policies can cause female employees, who have caregiving responsibilities, a lot of stress as they try to juggle the needs of their employer with the needs of their family. In this kind of environment, women with caregiving responsibilities can be viewed as less committed or less ambitious than their male counterparts, regardless of the quality of the work they produce. This, in turn, makes them less likely to be considered for senior roles.

Unconscious Gender Bias and How To Get Around It

On the whole, gender discrimination is something that most of us, even as women, can be unaware of. Part of the reason for that is our own unconscious bias. This bias is unconscious but strongly influences us when it comes to making decisions.

Research into cognitive bias has shown that we make conclusions about people very quickly, and most of our conclusions are based on our pre-programmed biases. Evidence of this can be found in the recruitment process, where both men and women have been shown to discriminate against female candidates for jobs or promotions without even realizing that they were doing it.

One such example in 1995 looked at a group of Swedish scientists. Researchers studied scientist's response to a selection of applications for research fellowships. Overwhelmingly, the scientists perceived women with the same number and level of accomplishment in the form of published scientific papers to be less competent than men with the same level of publications.

A simple change to anonymizing the applications by removing names removed the issue, and the candidates were then judged equally.

The unconscious nature of this bias makes it especially uncomfortable to address. People will vehemently deny that their behavior is biased because it isn't a conscious decision. Because of this, it can be uncomfortable to address. It can also lead to women silently suffer from the invisible barriers that can make them feel disconnected from their male colleagues and excluded from better roles and higher salaries.

So where does this unconscious bias come from?

It starts from very early childhood where we learn what activities, toys, and items are suitable for boys, and which are suitable for girls. Most children from age three or even earlier can apply a 'gender' to everyday items like dolls, make-up, and footballs.

So where do they learn this?

Everywhere. Television shows, books, adults, and other children are all constantly reinforcing gender rules and labels. Girls can wear dresses, but boys can't. Girls are not 'forbidden' to play football but children will rarely see this happening, and instead, they will see mostly, if not only, boys playing football. Commercials will show girls playing with dolls, and boys playing with train sets.

At the same time, more subtle gender rules about behavior are being reinforced. Boys are noisy, but girls should be quiet.

Of course, there are exceptions. Children will also be exposed to adults and other children who don't conform to all these rules and stereotypes. There are commercials showing both genders playing with items like building blocks and toy kitchens. There are television shows that have characters acting against stereotypes. Yet these are still the exception to the rule, and overwhelmingly children are still learning that there are significant differences between the genders.

Preschool children will usually choose to play with children of the same sex, where boys engage in more aggressive play involving physical contact, girls engage in more cooperative play. In larger groups, when boys do play with girls they show less aggression and more cooperation – and vice-versa.

In some senses, this early observation that there are differences between genders is natural and to be expected. What's important to take away is that there are differences between the genders, but the similarities far outweigh the differences. And not every person fits the societal norms. In fact, the very existence of gender expectations can cause harm. Consider the statistical fact that more men commit suicide. One common theory for this is that men are discouraged from opening up because talking about feelings is a 'female' behavior.

You may think, what's the harm? Perhaps girls naturally want to play with dolls, boys want to play with building blocks. However, the most recent research disagrees. Scientists are now leaning more heavily towards the conclusion that many perceived differences between men and women are heavily influenced by nurture, not nature.

Additionally, when you look at the skills these toys build in children, dolls teach nurturing and empathy, building blocks teach problem-solving and creativity. Are we doing girls a disservice by discouraging them from choosing toys that society considers to be masculine? And are we doing boys a disservice by discouraging them from developing nurturing and empathy skills?

We soak up these gender biases because they surround us.

Even if you don't agree with them, they are there in your subconscious. By the time we're ready to enter the workplace, we're already primed to consider men better leaders and women better secretaries – whether we realize it or not.

Linguistic Issues
Robin Lakoff investigated the idea of gender discrimination through language, and her findings were interesting. Lakoff concluded that men and women have different ways of expressing themselves through speech that add to the gender stereotypes that we see around us. In her book, *Language and Women's Place,* she suggested that one of the reasons women are perceived as weaker and less authoritative than men is down to the language they use.

She identified some linguistic behaviors that were more common among women than men, and that would add to this perception.

Women used exaggerated intonation that explicitly displays emotions like excitement, anger, and uncertainty. While men do use intonation, they were less likely to use it as often, or as exaggeratedly. By speaking in this way, others perceive women as more emotional – equaling a possible negative quality in the workplace.

Women also tended to seek approval for actions by tagging questions onto the end of requests or statements. Rather than directly stating, for example, 'I'm going out for lunch', women were more likely to say something like, 'I'm going out for lunch if that's ok?'

Another example is that women used a lot more hedging words. These are words and phrases like 'maybe' and 'just' that can indicate uncertainty or a lack of confidence in what you are saying. For example, whereas a man might say, 'I wanted to ask you a question," women are more likely to say, "I just wanted to ask you a question.'

Women are generally less direct in their speech, and more likely to give subtle (or not subtle) hints and cues that they want the listener to pick up on. They might say, 'It's a little hot in here', rather than, 'can you open a window?'

Women are more descriptive and use far more adjectives like 'lovely' and 'adorable.'

Women apologize more frequently and often apologize for the simple act of speaking or moving. Like this example – "I'm sorry, but I don't agree,"

Most of these examples illustrate how gender stereotypes displayed in language choices tell us that women should be polite, quiet, and unassertive. Women are less direct because they lack the innate feeling of authority to give instructions.

These are, of course, generalizations and women are perfectly capable of giving instructions, speaking directly, and keeping an unemotional tone. All of which are essential skills in leadership for specific situations. However, women show a distinct preference overall for speaking in a particular way that can unconsciously undermine their authority.

In-Group Favoritism
All humans have a natural preference for other people that are most like us. We prefer others who have a similar appearance to ourselves, and who have similar life

experiences and backgrounds. All friendships are formed based on some kind of common ground. We're naturally attracted to qualities in others that we see in ourselves.

It's an evolutionary bias, leftover from the days that humans lived in small tribes and outside tribes were a real potential threat. It's controlled by the more primitive part of our brain, and it's another unconscious bias that's fueled more by nature than by nurture.

Unfortunately, the implications are that we are more likely to hire and promote people who look, think, and behave as we do. When most leaders are still men, that unconscious bias serves to keep women out of leadership positions.

However, we've already shown that often even women will also favor a male candidate over a female one because of the unconscious gender biases that we all inherently carry. So why doesn't in-group favoritism win out in those situations?

In-group favoritism is a complicated bias. When we lived in small tribes, those tribes were naturally mixed gender. How we perceived 'otherness' wasn't limited to gender alone back then, and so it isn't only driven by gender today. Any time you identify yourself as in 'a group' you naturally begin to display biased behaviors where you favor people from that group.

The 'group' can be a literal group – classmates or a group of colleagues on a project. Or it can be a perceived group – people with similar hobbies, or even just people who wear the same brand of sneakers as you do. When faced with a choice, depending on which group you identify most strongly with, that bias will win out. So if a female hiring a manager identifies herself as in a group with her peers –

who happen to be mostly male, it can reduce or remove the in-group bias that might make her prefer the female candidate.

There's also the fact that in-group bias is much less pronounced when one group considers itself inferior to the other. The more strongly people identify with their group, and the more positive they feel about being part of that group, the more likely they are to display this type of bias. For groups who consider themselves superior, the in-group bias is strengthened.

As we've already seen, when it comes to leadership and the workplace, men are considered the superior group, even if this is an unconscious consideration. Which places women as the inferior group. Therefore, women in hiring positions are even less likely to display in-group favoritism based on their own gender.

In-group favoritism isn't a complete blocker to women's progression, and it isn't the only one – but that's partly the point. Combined with the other second-generation issues outlined in this chapter, it combines to make a perfect storm that keeps women behind invisible social and workplace barriers.

Exclusion From Professional Networks

A lot of job and promotion opportunities are linked to people's networks. As the adage goes, it's not what you know but who you know.

To start, the way men and women successfully network is different.

Men tend to have a very wide network but only a few close

connections. Whereas, a study found that female leaders with close ties to two or three other female leaders were more successful and benefited more from a smaller, closer network compared to their female counterparts who used a more male-dominated style of networking. Yet, the men who are part of the male-dominated networks are still much more successful than those more successful women in the study due to the better opportunities afforded by male networks.

And it's the exclusion from male-dominated networks that still very much hurt women's careers. Often women are unable to even join the networks and without access, some of the best jobs will always be just out of reach. Those jobs will be allocated without women even being considered for the roles. Even if we did somehow manage to get in, we still wouldn't get the same benefits as the males in the same network.

Another issue is that some male networking and business-related conversations often take place in venues that are inherently unwelcoming for women. Places like gentleman's clubs, golf courses or even more astounding, strip clubs, can be common places for males to meet male business clients or to discuss business with other men. These are intrinsically masculine places, which often make women feel uncomfortable, much less wish to conduct business negotiations or networking in these venues.

While women are not always explicitly excluded from entering these places, and indeed some women may particularly enjoy a round of golf, even there they are often segregated or differentiated in some way from the men – many clubs insist on different tees!

This is particularly common in industries like business to

business sales. It's often expected that a male client will be entertained in a venue like this. Even when women want to attend these venues with male colleagues, they are usually prevented from attending wherever possible.

Regardless of your moral stance on places like strip clubs, it's a reasonable assumption that organizations that allow and encourage business deals to be negotiated in them are openly discriminating against women.

Even where obvious exclusion due to venue choice isn't happening, women are still excluded both inside and outside of the workplace from men's social networks that offer those men a lot of valuable professional development opportunities.

Self-discrimination
We've touched on this several times in this chapter but it isn't only men that discriminate against women in the workplace. A number of the second generation issues are the result of masculine styles dominating businesses and organizations. As a result, those styles and expectations are being passed down and being held by lots of women too.

Some of the discrimination is from women who are naturally more masculine in their leadership style and have managed to reach a leadership position. Particularly in male-dominated industries, it's likely that they perceive themselves as part of the 'leadership' group of the industry and adopt the prevailing beliefs of that group-in-group favoritism in action. They are especially difficult to sway from their beliefs because if they managed to do it – why can't any woman intelligent and savvy enough follow in their footsteps?

Of course, not all female leaders hold this viewpoint, and plenty are true champions of gender equality but because of the unintentional nature of these particular biases, many women uphold them without even realizing it; as do many men.

Even more insidious is when women self-discriminate. You might question if that's even possible but human behavior is a complicated beast, and it's perfectly possible to sabotage your leadership career unconsciously.

Much of this is closely linked with mindset. It's becoming more and more recognized that the right mindset is the key to success but women in particular struggle with having the right mindset to set themselves up for that success.

Your mindset is made up of numerous internalized beliefs. Your concept of gender and gender rules and stereotypes are only part of your mindset. Your beliefs about money, power, leadership, and work that you've picked up both consciously and unconsciously over your lifetime all play into these beliefs.

The core problem of having a self-limiting mindset is that you naturally self-sabotage to validate your beliefs. People who want to earn a lot of money but have negative limiting beliefs about money, such as that rich people get richer and poor people stay poor, have a harder time motivating themselves to take the necessary action towards that goal.

Other people might believe that money only happens with hard work – the 60 hours plus work weeks and surviving on five hours of sleep a night kind of hard work. While hard work does usually pay off, that kind of working pattern will see most people fail from stress and exhaustion before they have a chance to reach their goals.

Women who hold limiting beliefs about their ability to lead – which may or may not be linked to their assumptions about gender – will always struggle to make progress.

A growth mindset is the most productive mindset, and it's also linked with a transformational leadership style – which we've already noted is the style most likely to lead to success.

A lot of deep-rooted self-limiting beliefs that hold women back in the workplace are linked to gender. Women might feel uncomfortable asking for a pay rise, and so find that they are not awarded anything because their manager has prioritized the department budget on those who did ask.

Women are taught that they shouldn't be too loud, shouldn't impose on others, shouldn't be pushy, shouldn't be greedy. While there are undoubtedly men that are brought up with the same beliefs, these particular limiting beliefs are almost always relevant to women.

These limiting beliefs can lead women to behave in the way they think they should, rather than how they want to behave. So they may give up work to raise a family when what they really wanted was to build a career alongside being a mother. Or they may not put themselves forward for promotions unless strongly encouraged, because they don't want to seem 'full of themselves.'

"I would venture to guess that Anon, who wrote so many poems without signing them, was often a woman."
Virginia Woolf, English writer.

Although plenty of women deny the existence of these second-generation issues, they are affecting the working lives of women in the Western world and beyond every day. Let's take a look at an example of a female professional who doesn't believe that she has experienced gender discrimination of any kind.

Real Life Case Study – Heather

Heather is a junior partner in a corporate law firm. As a lawyer, she's aware of gender and other forms of discrimination but firmly believes that she has not personally experienced gender discrimination. Heather graduated from an Ivy League law school. Her recollection of studying law there was that there were no differences in the treatment between the male and female students.

Heather chose corporate law, as this was the route she was encouraged down by her female careers advisor. She had considered litigation but her tutors and adviser felt that her skills matched better with corporate law. In fact, Heather can only remember one female student out the eighteen in her class opting to enter the litigation field.

Heather made junior partner after two years but she hasn't progressed since then. She points out that the only person to have progressed in that timeframe is her colleague Ben, and Heather admits he works longer hours than she does. Heather feels this isn't discriminatory because Heather is still unmarried and has no children – so her choice to work less than Ben is just evidence that he's more driven than she is.

In this case study, Heather denies that she's been subjected to discrimination of any kind. Yet between the lines of her story, there is evidence of unconscious biases. For example, women are often shepherded into particular educational/career choices.

When Heather's tutors encouraged her towards corporate law, chances are that they were encouraging all of the female students to go down that route. Why? Because of the unconscious gender bias that tells us women are not 'suitable' for litigation because they are too emotional or too 'soft' for trials. Society tells us that men are better at handling the pressure of litigation.

Undoubtedly, her tutor felt it was honest and genuine advice, and that it reflected her strengths based on assignment scores. Yet would her assignment scores have been the same if papers were marked anonymously?

Heather's lack of progression and her reasoning behind her male colleague deserving promotion more is also common. Heather feels that if she'd have worked longer hours, she might have been promoted. Yet she chose not to, and her colleague was promoted. Unfortunately, the acceptance of this kind of culture is still intrinsically detrimental to women. What if Heather does have children? Why are longer hours a sign of a better candidate? Surely performance is a better indicator of the right candidate?

Heather is optimistic about her chances for progression in the future. She points to the fact that there are women in two of the twelve senior leadership positions in the firm, whereas just ten years ago there were none. Surely, that's progress?

It's entirely possible that Heather will achieve her career ambitions. Many women can and do thrive in their careers – but when they do, it's against the invisible odds. The lack of women in high-level positions isn't a symptom of women's lack of ambition. It's second-generation gender issues.

Second generation issues can be difficult to spot, and it's even harder to get people to pay real attention to them. The gender discrimination cases we hear about are usually high-profile and blatantly obvious. Being dismissed for being pregnant would be obvious and easy grounds for a discrimination case.

Yet a recent UK survey highlighted that one in nine expectant mothers felt forced to leave their jobs. The majority of these were not dismissed or laid off. Instead, they believed they were being treated so unfairly that they had no choice but to leave. If that data was extrapolated, it could be assumed that over 50,000 pregnant women left the UK workforce because they felt forced and not because they chose to do so willingly.

In the next part of this book, we'll investigate how we define gender, look at gender stereotypes and identify what to expect if you choose to not conform to those stereotypes.

Chapter 4 – Gender, Equality and Getting Your Worth

"A gender-equal society would be one where the word 'gender' does not exist: where everyone can be themselves."
Gloria Steinem, American feminist, journalist, and social political activist.

Gender

We've talked a lot about gender so far but what does gender really mean? How did certain traits come to be defined as masculine or feminine? And how does the masculine vs. feminine debate impact leadership careers?

In this chapter, we'll explore and break down gender a little further and clarify some key concepts.

Masculine vs. Feminine

The words *'masculine'* and *'feminine'* usually conjure up certain images of men and women that fit stereotypes. But are these natural preconceptions, based on real biological and neurological differences between men and women? Or are they simply perceptions, constantly reinforced because of confirmation bias?

Of course, the concept of masculinity and femininity is related to certain behaviors rather than being biological constructs, although we tend to refer to physical features in this way too. Referring to a woman as masculine or a man as feminine is generally seen as an insult, a way to point them out as *'abnormal'* in the context of society as a whole.

To add to this, what's considered masculine and feminine varies between different cultures – indicating that what we perceive as masculine and feminine traits aren't biologically programmed but are instead influenced by what we see and hear around us. As such, they are generally learned attitudes and behaviors, a nurture issue rather than a nature one.

However, Neuroscientists have discovered that male and female brains do have some structural differences. For example, female brains have verbal centers on both the left and right hemispheres of the brain, whereas males only have a verbal center on the left hemisphere. Scientists believe that this is the reason that females tend to have more interest and skill in talking about feelings than males do.

Nonetheless, brains are still an individual quality, and these differences are very generalized. Male and female brains aren't like mass-produced items manufactured on a production line. While they are roughly uniform in size and function, there are numerous variables that can be different for every person regardless of their gender.

One recent study reported in *New Scientist* concluded that, *"averaged across many people, sex differences in brain structure do exist, but an individual brain is likely to be just that: individual, with a mix of features."* So there are neurological differences but these don't account for our perceived gender differences as much as we once thought.

What about hormones then, you may ask? Much is made of the effects that testosterone has on behaviors like competition and aggression but yet more recent research indicates that it isn't the magic potion that entirely explains masculine behaviors. While it is certainly linked to an increase in those behaviors, it isn't the singular driving force it has always been presumed to be.

Of course, our notions of competition and aggression are also cultural. Men and women can both be aggressive or competitive but the way they express that is often related to their culture's gender norms.

In the Western world, and many other developed countries, gender norms place men and women at polar opposites of the scale in terms of feelings, logic, practicality and nurturing. It's common in most cultures that women are perceived to be the ones in a partnership who will look after the home and children while a male partner goes to work.

Yet for all of society's insistence that men and women are very different, it's easy to overlook the fact that we're very similar. In psychology, there are five core personality traits: extraversion, openness, conscientiousness, neuroticism, and agreeableness. A study into how these traits varied between genders demonstrated that actually, there was less variance than expected. In fact, there was significant overlap between male and female participants.

Physically there are obvious differences in anatomy but psychologically we're much more alike than we are different.

<u>Definition of Gender</u>
The World Health Organization's definition of gender is: *"Gender refers to the socially constructed characteristics of women and men, such as norms, roles, and relationships of and between groups of women and men. It varies from society to society and can be changed."*

Gender is something of a loaded term. In the last few years, the concept of gender has been hotly debated. Challenges to our societal gender constructs have been more vocal. Many individuals feel that they don't 'fit' into the gender constructs that society has laid out for them and are pushing back against constructs that force them to choose if they are a 'man' or a 'woman.'

All too often, we confuse gender for sex. The sex of a person is generally determined by their genitalia and their genetic makeup – people with a 'Y' chromosome are considered male although there are rare genetic exceptions to even this 'rule'.

The gender of a person is a more abstract and fluid concept. It relates less to the biology of a person and more to the role of that person in society – how they identify and express themselves and how they are identified by others. It's possible to be born with both sets of genitalia, at which point in most countries the parents will choose which gender they assign to the child.

Gender Stereotypes and Roles
What is a gender stereotype? It's a preconception about attributes or characteristics of men and women; or about the roles that should be performed by women and men. They tend to be overly simplified, very generalized and very pervasive.

Gender roles are how society expects us to speak, behave, and look based on whether we're male or female. We've discussed at length so far what some of these expected roles and stereotypes are in the Western world. These stereotypes and roles are one reason why we still don't see many female engineers or airline pilots, or male childcare workers. If you ask a young child to draw a picture of a firefighter and a nurse, the chances are that the firefighter will be male and the nurse will be female.

But not only do these stereotypes vary across cultures, but they also vary over time and it's not always related to large social and political movements like women's rights. For example, you might be surprised to learn that as late as 1918, blue was considered a feminine color in the U.S. and pink was actually the more masculine color.

Even that pinnacle of stereotypical femininity, the high heel, was originally designed for men to wear while hunting on horseback. Over time, the style and design changed as women began wearing them, and as the high heel began to be associated more with femininity, men's shoes no longer incorporated such a high heel.

But are gender stereotypes really harmful? Many people will argue that these stereotypes exist precisely because they tend to be accurate, if generalized, reflections of how people of each gender dress, speak and behave.

The problem is that stereotypes are harmful when and if they place limits on both men and women's ability to make choices and pursue lives and careers that fit them as an individual. If a male is deterred from becoming a preschool teacher because it's a 'woman's' job then the stereotype is harmful. If a high school girl takes art instead of metalwork because 'metalwork is for boys' then it's harmful.

Negative stereotypes are the ones that are usually identified as harmful, such as women being over-emotional to the point of hysteria. Yet stereotypes that are presented as positives can still hold people back. Saying that women are caring and nurturing sounds like a good thing. Being caring and nurturing is a good thing, but it's not intrinsic to being a female.

However, that caring stereotype is one of the reasons that when an elderly relative needs care, it usually falls on the women in the family to pick it up. Men can and do take on caring responsibilities, but it's simply not expected that men will fulfill that role in the same way it is for women. This is all because of gender stereotypes.

For people in certain groups, like ethnic minorities or low economic status, the impact of existing gender stereotypes combined with other stereotypes for their groups can mean that they are even more heavily affected by the harmful effects of stereotyping.

On the surface, some stereotypes can seem harmless and even a little amusing, but recognizing all stereotypes for what they are and making an effort to look beyond them would result in a fairer and more comfortable world for most of us.

Questioning Femininity

"Always be a first-rate version of yourself instead of a second-rate version of somebody else."
Judy Garland, American singer, and actress.

We know that typically masculine traits are considered more desirable in leadership positions, and over the years women have received the advice to act more like men to get ahead. From wearing 1980's power suits with shoulder pads designed to give women a more masculine silhouette, to business coaches advising women to be me more masculine, the message has been 'if you can't beat them, join them'.

Studies have backed up this theory that masculine traits are more desirable in employees. In a 2017 experiment, researchers tested this theory by submitting graduate job applications across a wide range of sectors. Each application contained the same academic qualifications and experience but half emphasized masculine traits and hobbies like competitive sports and analytical thinking. The other half emphasized feminine traits and hobbies like embroidery and communication. The researchers found that the applications with masculine traits were 28% more likely to be invited to interview.

But what are the underlying issues and implications when women behave in a way that society deems masculine? Let's take a look at some examples of powerful women:

Hilary Clinton
The voting public usually expects all candidates to emulate strength and competence, which are two masculine traits. However, especially for women candidates, being too tough can lead to voters considering them to be insufficiently warm and engaging.

Over her career, Hilary developed a reputation for being 'too' ambitious. This is a criticism rarely aimed at men, whose ambition is often admired rather than criticized. In the media, everything from the shape of her mouth to the frequency with which she smiled was criticized.

Trump, as her political opponent frequently asserted that Hilary lacked the right 'temperament' or the stamina for the job of president. These accusations played heavily on the stereotypes of women as being overemotional, weak and fragile.

There's evidence that displaying masculine traits does cause female candidates to be less likable – but interestingly this effect is mostly confined to members of opposing parties. Their own parties are likely to view them more positively when they emphasize masculine traits.

Hilary's presidential campaign is a great example of in-group bias at play. Because of the context of the political arena, Democrats, on the whole, were great supporters of Hilary. Her party members viewed her as a strong and capable candidate. Republicans, however, found her less likable and not just because she was a Democrat. But because she was a woman behaving outside of expected gender norms. Had the Democrat candidate been a male, the chances are they would have been less strongly disliked or vilified by the opposition.

Margaret Thatcher
A remarkable woman, who was leading the UK at a time when female leaders were incredibly rare. She's often considered to have demonstrated many masculine traits, and famously had voice coaching in her early career to make her voice deeper – and therefore more authoritative.

Despite this, her political campaigning did quite often play to her feminine side. In one campaign she played to the housewife stereotype to appeal to female voters and potentially avoid the pitfalls of being labeled as 'too' masculine. In fact, she famously once said: *"perhaps it takes a housewife to see that Britain's national housekeeping is appalling."*

Although, she did not always conform to gender norms and was generally ambivalent about women's rights and feminism. Shortly after she gained leadership of the

Conservative Party, she was asked whether she saw it as a victory for women. She responded by saying, *"It is not a victory for women. It is a victory for someone in politics."*

Angela Merkel

In many ways, Angela Merkel has not overtly demonstrated masculine behaviors. If anything, she appears to have worked hard to present an image that is as gender-neutral as possible, while still identifying as a woman.

Still, she came under scrutiny early in her career for her frumpy exterior and sensible hair. She's usually seen wearing flat black shoes, pants and a suit jacket. It's difficult to imagine a male candidate coming under scrutiny for dressing in a sensible and tidy manner.

She's not entirely devoid of traits that could be considered masculine, however. She is considered ruthless when necessary, and particularly in her seizure of power in the wake of the scandal that saw her predecessor step down.

She also rarely, if ever displays any signs of emotion. It's her unruffled calm that makes her stand out when her male counterparts are allowing their emotions to get the better of them. This approach has worked very well. She's been leading Germany for well over a decade, and is generally well-liked and respected by voters and by her staff.

Golda Meir

Became Israel's first and only female prime minister in 1969. When questioned about how she felt becoming a female leader, she reacted in a similar way to Margaret Thatcher, responding, *"I don't know. I never was a man. This is who I am. Don't separate me as a woman. I am a person. I am a leader and that is how I should be seen."*

Despite her quote, David Ben-Gurion once famously said that Golda was, *"the only man in the cabinet,"* and Richard Nixon said of her, *"she acted like a man and wanted to be treated like a man."*

Again, like Margaret Thatcher, Golda Meir did not align herself with feminist groups and actively shunned them. The most likely reason for this is that she wanted to retain power in a political world that was still mostly dominated by men.

She was considered to be a strong personality with an indomitable will – generally masculine traits. However, Golda didn't hide her femininity and was not afraid to use it if she thought it would play to her advantage. She entertained foreign dignitaries in her kitchen, serving them home-cooked food while wearing an apron.

Despite initial popularity, the Yom Kippur war proved to be her downfall. Although under her leadership Israel won the war, the government was considered to have been unprepared and Golda was considered personally responsible for the deaths of thousands of Israeli men.

Several experts have posited that she was treated particularly harshly after the war because of her gender. Her decisiveness and actions were labeled 'arrogance' and people questioned how she could make military decisions having never been a general. Of course, as a woman at that time she was prohibited from serving in the army and so the underlying issue was at least partially one of gender, not specifically experience.

The examples of these women who have held some of the most powerful positions in the world show that it's possible to get ahead by embracing masculine traits but that there can be consequences. Arguably the most successful, Angela Merkel, adopts a more neutral approach rather than embodying either masculine or feminine traits.

Yet while women can get ahead by displaying masculine traits, there is a trade-off in terms of likeability. Society doesn't like it when people behave outside of their preconceived gender norms and so at best they have to find a way to justify it. At worst, they demonize it.

For the powerful women we've just discussed, people often justified their masculine traits by setting them apart from other women, as something 'other'. In some cases, even the leaders themselves avoided discussions of gender and steered conversations about their gender towards a more neutral approach.

However, none of them escaped scrutiny and sexist commentary. From the way they dressed to how they spoke, they have all at some point been scrutinized by the press and found wanting in some area of femininity. Interestingly, masculinity, whether it be lacking or overt, is something that you rarely have seen as being highlighted by the press in male leaders.

We know that masculine traits are more commonly associated with competence in the workplace, and an aura of competence is essential to be taken seriously as a leader. But we also know from studies that when people behave outside of gender expectations, then they instantly become less likable.

This puts women leaders in a double bind. They can behave in a masculine fashion and hopefully be seen as overall more competent, or they can be more widely liked and benefit from the advantages that brings. They usually can't have both. Even worse, there's no guarantee that they'll be successful regardless of which option they choose.

Overcoming Social Constructs and Constraints

In theory, women in the western world are not prohibited from entering any career field they choose. They can be engineers, leaders, judges, pharmacists, anything they want to be. However, women are still disproportionately represented in those roles. Why?

One reason is the pervasive gender stereotypes and roles that society place upon both genders. The only way to get beyond these is to slowly remove them, for both genders. The current problem is that one set of traits is seen as preferable to certain career choices, and we all feel invisible pressures to conform to our gender roles.

Then there's another aspect of the conversation. The possibility that perhaps women don't always want these traditionally masculine roles. Perhaps, goes the argument, many women gain more job satisfaction from traditionally 'feminine' roles, and will seek them out regardless. This is, indeed, possible. However, until we stop imposing gender norms, how can we quantify how many women choose these roles freely and how many choose these roles because they feel it's expected of them?

The key here is that there should always be a choice for anyone of any gender; a free choice unhindered by gender roles and expectations; a choice driven by the individual's wants, needs, and skills. The more we can steer ourselves and our organizations away from gender roles and expectations, the closer we will be to achieving equality. Yes, it's possible that given full equality, a majority of women will still choose roles in fields like education, arts and fewer will choose engineering or firefighting. But until the invisible barriers are lifted, we'll never know.

How and Why Should We Tackle These Issues?
We've spent a large part of the book so far looking at what issues women face, how these issues arose and how they impact women in the workplace as well as in society as a whole. This background information is necessary so that we all know what issues need to be overcome.

However, the fundamental question is what do we do about these issues? What can we do? What are the benefits of tackling these issues? In the next part of this book, we'll investigate how tackling these issues benefits everyone – not just women, and identify potential solutions to counter gender issues in the workplace.

Chapter 5 – Breaking Gender Barriers Down Fast

"The moral case for gender equality is obvious. It should not need any explanation."
Paul Polman, Business Leader.

Impact of Gender Barriers
Breaking down gender barriers doesn't just positively affect women, although, arguably it's women who stand to gain the most from a more equal society. However, gender stereotypes and roles can (and do!) have an adverse impact on men as well as women.

Let's consider for a moment the impact of gender stereotypes on men.

Men displaying traits associated with femininity can find themselves ridiculed, and men can feel just as much pressure to steer clear from careers traditionally associated with women. Men are often told that 'real' men don't cry. Crying is something that women do, a sign of their emotional instability and a sign of weakness. Yet in reality, crying is normal human behavior for both men and women. It's also a natural and powerful way to relieve emotional stress. Discouraging men from crying leaves them bottling up emotions that they're not sure how to express for fear of being seen as weak.

The flipside of men being the dominant gender in the workforce is that we tend to equate men's worth with their career. In particular, we associate their worth with their salary. High earning men are considered to be powerful. In contrast, women's worth tends to be tied to their looks or their nurturing abilities. Women are often left frustrated when their careers stall after childbirth. However, men feel immense pressure to be a suitable breadwinner in a household that's dropped from two incomes to one. It can also lead to men feeling embarrassed and emasculated if their female partner earns a higher income.

By breaking down gender barriers, we make strides towards a more just and equal society. Will it fix all of society's issues? No, but just like houses are built brick by brick, we need to lay the foundations of a just and equal society. Gender is one place to start.

Besides the altruistic reasons to promote more gender diverse workplaces, there are tangible business benefits to promoting diversity at work. Let's break down some of the key benefits that businesses can expect from becoming more gender diverse.

Benefits From Breaking Down Gender Stereotypes To Businesses And Organizations

"Women belong in all places where decisions are being made... It shouldn't be that women are the exception."
Ruth Bader Ginsburg, Associate justice of the U.S. Supreme Court.

Hire And Retain The Best People
Businesses exist for one reason – to make money and be successful. Even non-profits need to run their businesses effectively so that they can give more back to the groups that they are aiming to help.

To encourage better gender diversity, it's crucial that

businesses assess their hiring and promotion processes. These two processes are the biggest factor in promoting more diversity. Yet many companies still have hiring and promotion processes that put women at a distinct disadvantage. Unfortunately, this indirect discrimination against female candidates is also putting businesses at a distinct disadvantage.

Women make up half of the talent pool. Not only that, but according to the National Center for Education Statistics, they're the most qualified half. In the 2018-2019 academic year, women will earn over 57% of all awarded bachelor's degrees and over 51% of doctorates.

Women who do make it to the top of the corporate ladder tend to have more academic qualifications than their male colleagues. Yet, despite female graduates outnumbering men, they are less likely to be hired into entry-level jobs. At management-level jobs, this gap widens even further. Female candidates are much less likely to be hired into management level jobs. They are also much less likely to be promoted into them. Overall, only 38% of all management level positions are held by women.

If this doesn't change, the rate of growth in the number of women leaders is going to be painfully slow. When women are under-represented at every stage of the career ladder, it causes a knock-on effect of fewer women qualified to become C-suite leaders. Yet if companies start addressing these lower-level gaps now, we can close that gap much quicker.

More choice for women also means more candidate choices for businesses. In turn, this means that businesses can attract and retain the very best people for their organization. Creating career paths that are clearer, alongside working conditions less hostile to women, will allow women to be more motivated and driven to help the business succeed.

As we've discussed, there needs to be a focus on bottom-up hiring processes but there's also value in a focus on getting women into senior leadership roles. Once a business has recruited a good ratio of female leaders into its ranks, there's a trickle-down effect. Having more female senior leaders tends to lead to less gender discrimination in all recruitment processes in the business, including promotions.

Simply Having A Diversity Policy Can Make You More Attractive To Potential Employees. Millennials make up the largest segment of the workforce today. Research by UK consultancy PwC showed that over three-quarters of female millennials consider prospective employer's culture and their equality and diversity policies. In fact, 61% of women overall take into account the gender diversity of the leadership prospective employers when deciding where to work. By not having policies that promote diversity, you're potentially losing out on gaining some of the best talent.

It's important to note that a good hiring process doesn't mean favoring female candidates. It simply means that the process should encourage all candidates and allow the hiring manager to select the best person for the role. With that in mind, can any business really afford to discourage or ignore the most academically qualified half of the population when it comes to hiring?

Having a higher proportion of female leaders doesn't just lead to a better and more balanced recruitment process. It also leads to a lower staff turnover rate. Lower turnover is something that can save businesses a lot of money each year. When you're not spending large portions of your budget replacing staff who have left, you can concentrate on developing existing staff. This extra investment makes them more motivated and increases their loyalty and performance.

Higher Employee Engagement And Performance

It's a well-documented fact that employees who are more engaged with their organization are more productive, take fewer sick days and are better employees all around. As a result, most organizations place employee engagement high on their priority list.

Top business leaders understand that a high-performing workforce is essential for the growth of the business. The problem they face is how to achieve it. Regular surveys of employees give an indication of what can be improved but what is often overlooked is the importance of diverse workforces when it comes to engagement.

We've already covered how a lot of gender bias is unconscious and generally unintended – but that doesn't make it less harmful. When these biases go unnoticed, even by other women, it leaves us with a sense of unease. We know something isn't right, that we want something more from the organization's policies. Unfortunately, we aren't sure how to ask for it or even sometimes how to identify the problem. We don't feel fully engaged with the business but we don't know how to explain why.

Employee surveys have their place but results often show that people want more pay (not always possible across the board) and benefits. This results in employers introducing perks like free coffee, casual Fridays or employee competitions. These gimmicky solutions have a small place in engagement but they don't tend to drive real and sustainable engagement.

Studies have shown that a working environment that promotes diversity makes employees feel respected, engaged and involved with the business at a greater level. When this happens, employees are more productive and invested in their roles, and customers and clients receive better service.

Promote Creativity
Diversity also encourages collaboration, creativity and problem-solving – meaning you get more out of your employees. When diverse groups collaborate, the combination of unique perspectives leads to better ideas. The more diversity in a group, the more different perspectives can be considered. What's more, that feeling of inclusivity trickles down to your clients and customers making them more loyal to your brand.

In an interview with CNBC, Joe Carella, the assistant dean at the University of Arizona, Eller College of Management, confirmed that gender-diverse companies do become more creative. He said, *"We did our own analysis of Fortune 500 companies, and we found that companies that have women in top management roles experience what we call 'innovation intensity' and produce more patents — by an average of 20 percent more than teams with male leaders."*

There's lots of research demonstrating that diverse teams develop more innovative ideas. A diverse leadership team is more likely to promote an environment where ideas are shared, and creative ideas are considered. It's potentially down to the link between diversity and transformational leadership – which is also shown to encourage creative thinking.

However, to gain these benefits, your business needs to truly support and promote diversity. In order to contribute freely to discussions and generate innovative ideas and solutions, people need to feel safe and valued. If people don't feel safe to share their ideas or that their ideas are not valued by their peers and line management they will simply stop contributing.

It's not enough to just place more women in leadership positions. They need to feel safe and encouraged to contribute. When that happens, the boost to creativity can be remarkable.

Drive Business Profits and Performance
Having a gender-diverse business directly relates to having a more successful business. If business owners have been wondering why they should bother encouraging diversity then this is potentially the most compelling reason. If you're running a business, a healthier bottom line is always your key objective.

In fact, a McKinsey & Company report calculated that increasing gender diversity in the workplace could add $12 trillion to the global economy. Further research by McKinsey & Company demonstrated that businesses with a healthy balance of men and women are 15% more likely to outperform their competitors.

Clearly, the reasons for businesses to take gender diversity seriously are about more than just fairness and equality. Gender diversity isn't just a tick in the politically correct box: it's a competitive financial strategy.

Not convinced? A five-year study conducted by MSCI Inc into the performance of companies in the USA had some interesting insights. They found that businesses with a minimum of three women on the board had 45% higher earnings per share compared to those with none between

2011 and 2016.

A further Gallup study across two industries investigated over 800 business units. They discovered that gender-diverse business units generated an average of 14% more revenue and a 19% higher quarterly net profit than those with less diversity.

In yet another study, Harvard Kennedy School investigated employee gender in relation to sales and profits. They demonstrated that teams with an equal gender mix perform better than male-dominated teams in terms of sales and profits. They noted that sales and profits continued to increase proportionately in relation to the percentage of women, up to 50%. For teams with a higher proportion of women, there wasn't a decrease in performance compared to teams who were mostly male. However, they performed around the same level as the teams with an equal gender mix. What's especially interesting here is that the study looked at the performance of sales teams – which are typically male-dominated.

The relationship between high-performing companies and companies with a high percentage of female leaders is eye-opening. Research by the Peterson Institute for International Economics demonstrated that there is a correlation between higher profits and the number of women at the C-Suite. Companies with 30% or more leadership positions filled by women had at least 1% higher net profit margin when compared to companies without female leaders.

The amount of research demonstrating the relationship between a diverse leadership team and higher profit is staggering.

So why do the more diverse businesses perform better?

It's not necessarily true that women are better leaders but having more diversity at the decision-making level helps businesses perform better. In-group bias hurts business bottom-lines, and it's been demonstrated repeatedly that cultural diversity, as well as gender diversity, improves performance overall.

Without diversity at a senior level, a poor retention rate and disengaged employees could be the least of your issues. Shortly after the financial crisis, Sallie Krawcheck, co-founder and CEO of Ellevest and a former executive at Morgan Stanley and Citibank, blamed Wall Street's issue with 'groupthink' for contributing to the crisis. In an interview with CBS, she said: *"There was no doubt that had we had more diversity of thought, perspective, education, gender, color, the crisis would have been less severe."* She might have a point. In fact, after Iceland's banking crisis, the only bank left standing was headed by female leaders.

Attract Investors
In the same way that having a gender-diverse workforce and robust diversity policies can help you attract the best talent, they can also help you attract good investors. Several studies have highlighted that companies who adopt best practice policies, like a hiring process that encourages diversity, are seen as more attractive to investors. There's even research to suggest that when a business wins an award related to diversity, their stock prices increase.

However, there are caveats to this. An analysis of the research demonstrates that the industry context plays a large part in how much diversity affects investors. For industries that are traditionally male-dominated and less liberal culturally, the effect is diminished. For industries that are more liberal and aware of the benefits of promoting diversity, the effect is increased.

Having a gender-diverse workforce can positively impact how investors view the business and is highly unlikely to have any negative impact. As such, for businesses that haven't already done so, it makes excellent business sense to implement diversity policies as soon as possible.

The Vital Moves

Despite all the research showing the benefits, the academic performance of female students and the fact that it's the 21st century, many industries continue to be male-dominated. It's particularly obvious at the leadership level. Even now, 84% of engineers and architects are men, and computing isn't far behind.

The rise in numbers of women leaders is still slow, and even the companies that have gender-diversity policies and programs are not seeing the level of growth needed. But why?

In order to implement a successful gender diversity program, there needs to be a genuine desire to support women's leadership roles. All too often, businesses believe that hiring a token woman or two and paying lip service to gender diversity will 'solve the problem'. Unfortunately, this can create more problems than it solves.

As we've seen in earlier chapters, when women are placed into a male-dominated group, they too can begin to display in-group bias. Women who are the only females in a male-dominated leadership environment have a much harder time than when there is a true balance. They feel more pressure to fit in with male colleagues, and both they and the business they work for are less likely to experience the benefits associated with gender-diverse workplaces.

In contrast, when there are several female leaders at a senior level the real benefits of gender diversity begin to show. There's more collaboration, co-operation and a real embedding of gender diversity into the business culture.

Gender diversity is about more than meaningless quotas. In fact, a quota policy can breed distrust and resentment. Male colleagues can begin to feel that they are disadvantaged if there's an open quota to be filled. It can mean that even when women are promoted or hired on merit alone, they feel they have to work twice as hard to 'prove' that they deserve the role.

In contrast, when hiring and promotion policies are carefully reviewed to remove unconscious biases and barriers to female applicants, there will naturally be more successful female candidates. When it's clear that all roles are filled based on fair and robust criteria that don't disadvantage either gender, every successful candidate can begin their new role with the respect and support of all of their colleagues. It's important to promote the equality aspect – female-dominated departments can often benefit from more gender diversity as well.

Business leaders need to lead by example, promoting a culture of inclusion and open discussion. This way, all employees can raise concerns and have some input into how the business hires and promotes the best possible talent.

Real Life Case Study – David

David is the CEO of a large marketing consultancy. While his company continually made a profit, the level of profit had been stagnant year-on-year. Understandably, David wanted to drive the business to higher levels of success.

When his HR director presented him with a report citing research from Credit Suisse demonstrating an 18% return-on-investment premium for gender-diverse leadership teams, David knew he needed to pay attention.

Working closely with his HR team, David laid out his goals on achieving gender diversity in the business. His aim was to have a minimum of 30% of female leaders in the C-suite over the next five years. He also aimed to have all business departments with at least 40% of female employees.

To discover the best way to get the business there, David held a meeting with all of his current female employees to understand what barriers they faced, and how to remove them. His meeting uncovered that his female employees felt that the culture of long working hours was holding them back. Even if they produced the same amount and quality of work as employees who worked longer hours, his employees with caring responsibilities felt overlooked for recognition and promotion opportunities.

He also uncovered that there was a prevailing sense among female employees that the C-suite would be an unwelcoming environment for a female. When David asked why the employees felt the way, they mentioned that there was only one female leader out of nine board members.

David's first step was introducing a reward and recognition scheme that rewarded employees for high-quality work rather than excessive working hours. This immediate change addressed some of his employee's concerns about how the company valued employees with caring responsibilities.

His next step was to overhaul the hiring and promotion processes. Alongside his HR team, David reviewed the end to end process, from guidelines for placing an advertisement to how candidates were shortlisted. David took a radical approach. He suggested that all candidates who met the academic qualifications criteria were to be entered into a database. Via this database, the hiring managers could see the person's experience and qualification, but could not view the applicant's name, age, or gender. Based on this information, they could select the candidates for interview, who would be invited by the HR team.

By removing obvious identifiers of age or gender, David was removing a potential barrier for progressing female applicants. Each applicant could be judged on merit alone, making it more likely that a fair and diverse mix of candidates would be invited to interview.

Besides this radical change, they also removed any unnecessary insistence on inflexible working schedules. They also published their commitment to gender diversity on their corporate website and at the bottom of any literature relating to their hiring and promotions process.

The changes David implemented took over twelve months in total to embed and to begin to make a real difference. Over a 24 month period, the business saw a 10% increase of female employees at all levels and a 16% increase in the number of women promoted to a management level position. Over the same 24 month period, net profits rose by 4%, with projections for the following year being a total 6% increase.

So, we've covered why businesses should make an effort to break down gender barriers but how can everyone contribute to the cause? In the next chapter, we'll take a look at what individuals can do to promote gender equality in a positive way.

Chapter 6 – Your Own Choices

"We need women at all levels, including the top, to change the dynamic, reshape the conversation, to make sure women's voices are heard and heeded, not overlooked and ignored."
Sheryl Sandberg, American technology executive, author, and billionaire.

We've looked at the many ways that women are being held back in the workplace. While it's good to understand the background and why change needs to happen, what's even more important is to understand that you can also be a driver for change.

This book is all about empowering women to reach their potential in the workplace. It's about providing actionable advice for female leaders and aspiring leaders to implement. It's also to provide insights for hiring managers to improve gender diversity in their organizations.

So, with that in mind, let's take a look at what we can all do as individuals to improve the situation – for ourselves and for all women.

Achieving Confidence and Assertiveness

"It's not your job to like me, it's mine."
Byron Katie, American speaker and author.

We've discussed a lot of external factors preventing women from meeting their true potential in the workplace. Yet those barriers aren't the only thing holding women back. Sometimes, it's as much about mindset as it is about the environment that we work in.

Of course, the two things are linked. Your mindset is often heavily influenced by societal norms and what you perceive to be the truth of the way the world works. The barriers we've discussed so far influence your mindset without a doubt.

Luckily, your mindset is not a fixed thing. By recognizing issues as they arise and challenging your thinking and behavior, you can build a new more positive mindset that sets you up for success regardless of gender.

Change The Words You Use
Words hold a lot of power, and the words we use can shape other people's perceptions of us. With this in mind, it makes sense to be careful with the words we use about ourselves and others.

Women have a greater tendency to be self-deprecating, dismissive of praise, and overly polite or apologetic when asking for something or giving instruction. Perhaps it's because we believe that if we're straightforward, we might be labeled as 'a bitch' or overbearing. Yet men rarely make apologies simply for stating their opinion or asking a question, and this makes them appear more self-assured.

Women use a lot of filler words to soften their language. These are words and phrases like 'just', 'you see', and 'sort of'. When they're frequently used, they make the speaker sound unsure and unconfident.

Women are also more frequently apologetic. This can be a strength when used appropriately but when you're apologizing for having an opinion or daring to exist, then it is most certainly a weakness. By apologizing too much, and for the wrong things, you seem uncertain and weak.

Closely linked to being apologetic is the tendency to seek approval for ideas. Women are more likely to seek validation, whereas men are more likely to state their idea with the presumption that it will be challenged if it's not correct.

Women present their ideas in a manner that opens the idea up for criticism immediately. We invite and expect criticism rather than presenting the idea as though we expect it to be considered. The ability to accept criticism is an essential leadership skill but entering into every conversation expecting and inviting it is a different matter entirely.

Be More Confident
Self-doubt isn't an exclusively female trait but it is one that seems to plague many more women than men. On average, women gain more academic qualifications than men and earn higher grades, so why is that achievement not boosting women's confidence in their abilities?

We've previously looked at barriers in the workplace and society for women. In some cases, it's also this severe lack of confidence that's holding women back. Removing the barriers to promotion won't help if women won't put themselves forward for opportunities.

One study by Hewlett-Packard demonstrated that women would normally only apply for a position if they met 100% of the job requirements. For men, the threshold was 60%.

Women are more likely than men to believe they were 'lucky' to get a job offer or a promotion – even if their resume shows they are highly qualified for the role.

Women are also more likely to question their abilities and suffer from 'Imposter Syndrome'.

Sheryl Sandberg, Facebook's COO has been quoted as saying, *"There are still days I wake up feeling like a fraud, not sure I should be where I am."*

Women are less likely to ask for a pay rise or a promotion. Instead, they put all their effort into their work and hope to be noticed and rewarded for an excellent performance. In the meantime, their male colleagues are more likely to ask for what they want directly – and consequently more likely to get it. Even when women do negotiate salary increases, they set their sights approximately 30% lower than men do, which means even when they do ask, they generally receive less.

It's a proven fact that self-confidence and appearing confident are important factors leading to success. Confidence can be equal to competence when it comes to achieving career success. So, it's vital that women start to believe in themselves and their abilities.

One thing that holds women back from being more confident is the fear that they might be seen as arrogant if they have the same unshakeable self-confidence that a lot of male leaders seem to exude. However, confidence is very different from arrogance. Taking steps to be more assertive can help you come across as more confident – without appearing arrogant.

Be Assertive
Assertive behavior is a key leadership skill, regardless of gender. However, women often have a harder time displaying assertive traits because they tend to be perceived as 'male' traits. Women can sometimes shy away from

being assertive in case they are perceived as 'bossy' or 'aggressive'. However, a lot of assertive traits are quite 'female'.

Being assertive is very different from being bossy, arrogant, or aggressive, and it's something that all leaders should be aiming to develop. Assertive leaders express their thoughts and their feelings in a direct, honest, and appropriate way. Because of this, they often gain the trust and respect of their teams and their peers.

Assertive leaders are collaborative. They listen and respect the thoughts and feelings of others – a trait more often associated with women.

Assertion is closely linked to communication skills, something that women tend to be good at. Where women sometimes fall is in how clearly they communicate their own needs and goals. Adopting an assertive communication style when discussing promotion opportunities and pay rises can help you come across more confidently and authoritatively.

When assertive people discuss opportunities, they usually present clear and succinct evidence to back up why they should be considered for a promotion or pay increase. By calmly and clearly stating their case, they make it easy for their line manager to both understand what is being requested, and why they should consider it.

Assertive people tend to know their worth, and they accept that another person's opinion of them does not define them as a person. This might seem counter-intuitive to the idea that a good leader needs to have a certain 'image'. However, an assertive approach accepts that not everyone will like you or agree with you. Assertive leaders listen and take other's opinions on board. They might change their own opinion based on the argument of another person but they never back down out of fear or rejection because they know they are worth more than that.

Being assertive offers many benefits. By learning to be more assertive, you can effectively express your feelings in a way that others can understand. It allows you to be clear about what your needs are so that others can meet them.

It also helps you keep people from taking advantage of you, and ensures that your opinions are heard. Behaving assertively can help you gain the respect of others, and in turn, improve your confidence and self-esteem.

Need a quick way to become more assertive immediately? – Stand up!

A study from Washington University showed that simply standing up can make you automatically more assertive. They noted that when people stand up or move around more, they are also more creative and collaborative. According to another study by Stanford, a brief walk also boosted creativity, which is linked to assertion. To reap the benefits, try and move or stand more during the working day.

Ditch Perfectionism and Trying To 'Have It All'

"It is impossible to live without failing at something, unless you live so cautiously that you might as well not have lived at all – in which case, you fail by default."

J. K. Rowling, British novelist.

Perfectionism is something that plagues women. For some reason, women believe they need to be as perfect as possible. It's not uncommon for women to triple-check every report they send and beat themselves up mentally if they miss a typo. Many women will avoid putting forward an opinion in a meeting unless they're sure they understand the topic as well as an expert.

There's a damaging ideal that exists of the woman who 'has it all'. You know the one, the woman holding down a prestigious high-level management role. She has several perfectly well-adjusted children, a perfect home, holds regular dinner parties, and never has a hair out of place.

The thing is, she doesn't exist, and women need to stop trying to be her. Sure, there might be days or weeks when women can meet these exacting standards we set for ourselves but it's just not sustainable, or good for mental health, in the long term.

Am I telling you to stop trying to achieve big things at work and home? Not at all. It's important to understand the difference between aiming big and perfectionism.

This advice isn't to stop dreaming big, aiming high, and wanting to be the best you can be at everything. In fact, that's the point. Aim high, dream big. Be the best you can be.

If you're struggling and making compromises to hold down a career and a family, that's ok. You're not failing. By all means, look for solutions and improve your situation. But don't put yourself down because you're holding yourself to an impossible ideal and feel like you are 'failing' that ideal.

Social media makes this type of perfectionism even worse. Depending on who you have on your social media feeds, you might be overwhelmed with images of women who are 'perfect'. They seem to have perfect families, perfect make-up, perfect bodies. The problem is that it's easy to manipulate the image we present on social media. Just because somebody's life appears to be a certain way, doesn't make it that way in real life.

Stop comparing yourself, stop trying to uphold an unrealistic image of yourself. Aim high but accept that failure and setbacks are part of life for everybody. With an assertive, positive mindset you will begin to look at these as opportunities to learn and improve. Letting go of perfectionism allows you to take more action, get more done, and potentially make more progress in your career.

Create 'Me' Time To Grow And Nurture Yourself

It's important to take time out for self-development and self-care. What that looks like can be different for every individual but the key is to create the time, protect it, and use it in the best possible way.

It might be meditation; it might be time to reflect, plan, and set goals for yourself. It might be a spa day. It could be time to complete online courses or time to attend a night class. Whatever energizes you and helps you grow as a leader.

We live in a culture where hard work and long hours are seen as the ultimate keys to success. There's nothing wrong with hard work but working smarter and not needing to work excessive hours is a much better way. Unfortunately, our obsession with being productive and working long hours means we end up exhausted and burned out –

regardless of gender. And if you happen to have caring responsibilities like the majority of women, then getting everything done can seem overwhelming.

Taking time out to develop yourself or to practice self-care can seem like an indulgence you can't afford. In reality, it's a necessity you can't afford to ignore. When you're energized and well-rested, you can bring the best possible version of you to work. Investing time and effort in developing your knowledge and skills gives you the confidence boost to present the kind of self-assured persona that we already know contributes to success.

Stop putting yourself last on the list and secretly hoping someone will notice and give you a break. Give yourself a break and demonstrate that you value yourself. It won't be long before others pick up on the energy and start to recognize your value too.

Building Your Tribe

All the above are things you can do alone to develop the right mindset for success. The following suggestions are things you can do to get the support you need to succeed. These relate to building your authority as a female leader or entrepreneur and finding yourself a 'tribe' of like-minded women to support and encourage each other. We're keeping them in the 'what you can do alone' chapter because we're focusing on your specific part in joining and creating this tribe.

Embrace Your Femininity
We know that simply behaving like a man doesn't usually work for women in the workplace. While there are certain

lessons we can learn from the way men tend to do things; being more confident and less perfectionist, behaving in a way that feels unnatural will come across as untrue to others and might even make you unhappy.

For many reasons, women, in general, have a different perspective on life than men. This is a huge generalization but it holds true in many areas. Instead of seeing this a weakness, or focusing on negative differences, we can embrace the diversity of thought this brings, and use it to our advantage.

We already know that diverse workplaces are more creative, productive, and profitable – and it's all down to having a mix of perspectives and opinions to be considered. When management meetings and board meetings have a diverse range of people in them, the decisions made usually better reflect the needs of the end client or consumer.

So instead of agreeing with male colleagues for the sake of it or censoring your opinions because you're worried that they might be 'too' something – too emotional, too loud, too different, put your thoughts and opinions out there with confidence. If people don't agree that's fine but why not share what you have to offer and keep on doing it?

For example, when faced with handling a difficult member of staff, embrace your natural ability to empathize and listen. Use it to persuade the member of staff to change their behavior.

Not all women (or men) have the same innate traits, and that's absolutely as it should be. What I'm advocating here is that you embrace you. Allow yourself to express your opinions and handle situations in a way that makes the best use of your strengths – instead of trying to fit a mold made for somebody else.

Build A Network
Networks are essential for success but when women try to build a network in the same way as men, it doesn't give them the same success. So what's different about the way men and women network?

Men have broader networks, filled with casual relationships, whereas women tend to cultivate smaller networks with deeper relationships. Because men have wider networks, they can access more opportunities through that network. However, it's not all bad news for women.

The deeper relationships that women build can be very supportive, and when opportunities do arise, their network contacts are more likely to champion them for the role. Studies have shown that when women build networks that include other successful women, they achieve greater success than women who adopt a broader network in the style of male colleagues.

This doesn't mean you need a women-only network and that you should avoid networking with men. However, it does mean that you probably don't want to follow the same networking strategy as men. Ideally, you should seek to have as many successful and ambitious women in your network as possible.

Obviously, there are a lot fewer female leaders than there are male leaders, so alongside building your in-person network, taking advantage of online networks can give your career a boost.

Online networks like Girlboss gives you access to other

professionals, and with a female-heavy population, Girlboss is a great place to start. Despite the name, it's not a female-only network but it's the positive message of female empowerment attracts some of the best and brightest female talent.

Founded by Sophia Amoruso, a seriously successful serial entrepreneur, Girlboss aims to fill the gap that more traditional online networking sites like LinkedIn haven't managed to address. And alongside the networking aspect, there are also educational tools like podcasts and conferences aimed towards empowering more female leaders.

Networking, whether in-person or online, can be a very powerful career tool. It doesn't come naturally to everybody, and in-person networking can sometimes seem intimidating if you're not naturally self-assured.

One way to overcome this is to look at networking for what it is: building relationships. You can network at the coffee shop, the school gates, in the supermarket… Anywhere there are people you can speak to, you can network. Strike up a conversation wherever you're comfortable and find out about people. Some of the most interesting contacts can come out of the simple small talk struck up in unlikely networking places.

When you identify that someone might be a good addition to your network, hand them a business card, and schedule a follow-up meeting. The follow-up doesn't have to be formal, a casual conversation over coffee can be the perfect follow-up.

Networking events and groups are a better way to immediately connect with other professionals but beware that they can be intimidating at first. To take away some of the trepidation, prepare your 'elevator pitch' in advance and practice saying it out loud. That way, when you're inevitably asked, 'what do you do?', you'll be able to respond without nerves getting in the way.

Some cities even host female-only networking groups, which many women may find a more comfortable environment. Check for these being advertised on LinkedIn or other social media.

Look For An In-House Sponsor
Having a sponsor can give your career a real boost. It's important to note that a sponsor is different than a mentor. Mentors are excellent for advising you and guiding you in your career. A sponsor, however, is your own personal champion.

Mentors are also important to provide advice and support. Ideally, your mentor should be at the next step in their career compared to you. This way, they still understand the challenges you face at your current level, as well as being able to prepare you for the challenges the next level will bring.

You're not limited to just one mentor. You can have several but ideally with different experience and strengths so that you can learn from each of them differently. Lots of companies have a program to match you with a mentor but if your organization doesn't have one, it's worth seeking out a mentor on your own.

It's possible for someone to be both your mentor and your sponsor but the roles are very different. A sponsor doesn't always offer the same kind of support that a mentor does and vice versa.

Sponsors can help you bridge the gap from operation management to strategic management – something that many women can struggle with. A sponsor is always someone at least one management level above you. The idea is that they are championing you behind doors that are usually closed to you, like in board meetings.

A sponsor can put your name forward for big projects, promotions, and any opportunities that come up that might further your career. Because of this, your sponsor should be as senior as possible. Because they need to be able to get behind all of the organizational doors that are closed to you, the more senior and influential they are, the better.

Your sponsor doesn't have to be female. In fact, given the lack of females in high-level leadership roles, you may not be able to find a female sponsor within your organization. However, if you can find a female sponsor, then that's another great way to include successful females in your network.

Organizations don't usually offer programs to find a sponsor as they do with mentors, so it will be up to you to identify a build a relationship with a suitable sponsor.

<u>Become A Subject Matter Expert And Thought Leader</u>
We already know that women do better academically than men but then why are so many 'experts' in the press and on television men? That's not to say men can't be experts but it seems very disproportionate given that, statistically, men don't achieve higher grades academically.

Mostly, it stems from the self-confidence issue, coupled with the invisible barriers we've discussed in previous chapters. But it's time women stood up and claimed their expertise.

So, what is a subject matter expert? It's someone who knows more than most people about a topic. You don't have to know every single detail about the topic to be an expert but you do need to have a deep understanding of it.

Obviously, context matters. You can't enjoy reading articles and books on neuroscience and then set yourself up as an 'expert' in it without a formal education. Even if you do have excellent knowledge on the topic from self-study, academic expertise often requires academic qualifications and even potentially requires tenured experience.

If, however, you're the go-to person in your organization if someone wants to know about the tender process for procurement, then you're probably a subject matter expert. Identify a topic where your knowledge and experience exceeds the knowledge and experience of other individuals in your organization, and that's where you're potentially an expert.

Being an expert usually involves not just knowing about something but also having applied that knowledge in some way in the real world – ideally with some kind of proven results. Often, women do have the expertise, even including the academic qualifications to back that up – and yet don't claim that expertise.

If you know about a topic relevant to your company or industry, and you find people coming to you for help and advice – own it, build on it and celebrate it. You're a subject matter expert.

Once you're recognized as a subject matter expert on something, you can leverage your knowledge and expertise to become a thought leader. Thought leaders use their expertise to devise strategies and identify potential issues that can be avoided. For example, your expertise might be in marketing. You can be a thought leader by using your knowledge of up-and-coming marketing technology and trends to identify good areas for your organization to invest in – and avoid areas that you believe won't be as successful.

Depending on your subject, you could write an article on your area of expertise and maybe even pitch it to a big publication. Not a big writer? Appear as a guest on podcasts, attend business networking focus groups to talk about it. If it's limited to your particular organization, why not create a company Wiki on the topic or a training manual for others?

Find ways to leverage the knowledge you have, along with ways of building on that knowledge – and share it with the world, or at least your colleagues. You'll gain recognition and respect that are natural springboards into leadership.

Use Feedforward
Feedforward is a great feedback tool for all leaders but it can be put to particularly good use for female leaders looking to improve how others perceive them.

Asking for feedback can be a nerve-wrecking experience no matter your managerial level, and giving feedback to people more senior than you can also be nerve-wrecking. Feedforward can make it easier for both parties.

If you're not familiar with the concept, here's how feedforward works:
1. Choose a behavior that you want to change. It could be to contribute more often in meetings or to stop

using overly apologetic language.
2. Explain your goal to a colleague in a one-to-one setting.
3. Ask the person if they have two ideas on how you can achieve your goal, and listen attentively to their response. You are not allowed to challenge their response, simply listen. The only response you are allowed to give is 'thank you'.
4. Once you've done this, you repeat the same process with a different person.

So, why does it work better than more traditional methods of feedback? Marshall Goldsmith, the creator of the feedforward method, suggests that this method feels less uncomfortable, and therefore is easier to initiate. It also feels less intense, as you're not specifically asking people for their opinions on you, per se.

You're asking a general question on how you can reach a specific goal. Their advice is likely to take into account how they perceive you, so it's personal and specific advice. You receive the information you need without openly seeking criticism or having the information framed in a way that is likely to make anyone uncomfortable.

It's also a great way to focus on the future. Traditional feedback is, by nature, quite focused on your past behaviors. While you can learn a lot from your past behaviors, dwelling on what you did before is much less helpful than focusing on what you can do in the future.

Be Heard
If there's one thing every woman should at least try to do, it's to speak up. If you come across gender bias, call it out. You don't have to be confrontational about it. Handle it in a way that feels comfortable for you but don't let it slip by

unchecked.

Unfortunately, speaking up won't always help if you're not being heard. So how do you make sure that you're being heard?

Consider forming amplification groups with like-minded female colleagues. The concept of amplification emerged after a former female White House official confided to journalists that women in the White House had at times found it so difficult to be heard that they created amplification groups.

The purpose of amplification was for the women in the White House to literally 'amplify' other women's comments and ideas by repeating them and backing them. If a woman offered a comment or idea that was ignored in a meeting, another woman would repeat it, crediting the original woman who offered it. By doing this, it became very difficult for women's ideas to go unheard.

By forming amplification groups, and making use of all potential amplifiers, not only can women join together to call out gender-biased policies and practices, they can ensure that they are heard.

It's a cliché, but it's true. We need to become the change that we want to see. Applying these ideas to your own life can help you make personal progress towards becoming a great leader regardless of gender.

However, there's also a lot that women can do together. In the next chapter, we'll investigate some broad-based strategies that can help push change faster and further.

Chapter 7 – Broader Strategies For Everyday Use

"The women who have achieved success in the various fields of labour have won the victory for us, but unless we all follow up and press onward the advantage will be lost. Yesterday's successes will not do for today!"
Nellie McClung, Canadian author, social activist, suffragette, and politician.

The Case We Must Make

We've looked fairly closely at what individual women can do to address gender bias in the workplace, including building networks and joining together to form amplification groups. However, these strategies are very small scale.

These individual actions do make a difference. However, for real and effective change, it's going to take a combination of individual and collective actions, including broad-based strategies that businesses can implement.

Inclusivity Starts With The Hiring Process
It's probably stating the obvious that companies need to hire more women into senior roles, or roles that are likely to lead to senior positions in the future.

It makes sense to review hiring processes to ensure that they're as fair and robust as possible. Staff costs are usually one of the highest costs that any business bears and getting it wrong can be expensive.

Reviewing hiring processes to ensure that your company is hiring the best person for the role means successful candidates are more likely to stay with the business for longer. Your business gets better results and saves money on rehiring for the same role.

So what are some changes that you can implement to help eliminate gender bias from the hiring process?

Remove Identifying Details At Application
Consider removing identifying details from applications at the review stage. When the hiring managers can't see factors like names and ages, it's much harder for unconscious bias to creep in.

Your assessment and interview processes should be set up to support hiring managers to identify the best candidate for the role. All interview questions should be vetted to make sure there are no hidden gender biases.

Obviously, it's difficult to conceal gender at an interview. Interviewing managers should be trained in unconscious biases and experienced at hiring diverse people. Where the hiring manager lacks this experience, provide training and have them supported by an appropriate person who does have experience.

Your interviewers should be as diverse as possible so that in-group biases don't easily win out. Wherever possible:

Offer Equal Pay For Equal Work

"I may sometimes be willing to teach for nothing, but if paid at all, I shall never do a man's work for less than a man's pay."
Clara Barton, founder of the American Red Cross.

When establishing an appropriate starting salary, it's particularly important to make sure that you're not offering a lower rate to female candidates than an equally experienced male candidate. The starting salary should be commensurate with the role responsibilities. A candidate's previous salary history should not influence the salary you offer. Otherwise, you're potentially carrying over gender bias from other businesses into your own.

Your equal pay policy shouldn't end with new recruits. Existing gaps should be addressed, and salaries should be regularly reviewed to ensure that disparity hasn't been introduced over time as people receive performance-related pay rises and promotions.

Of course, the disparity in pay often first occurs when a woman decides to start a family. Creating more flexible working options for all employees including remote working, job shares, and consulting assignments will help you retain more women. It also prevents depreciation in salary because of a need to pause or step down in their career to accommodate family responsibilities.

It's important that all employees have the option for these benefits. While it can help to offer female employees more flexibility, if the same opportunities are not extended to male colleagues or colleagues without children, it can create hostility.

Design Roles Around People
Hire smart, capable people and design the role around them. What is often overlooked is that it's not enough to just change the hiring processes. You also need to change the roles you're hiring into. Trying to shoehorn women into roles that have been designed with men in mind – whether

consciously or not – isn't going to work.

The traditional hiring process is seldom questioned. Companies decide what they need, create a job role, and then hire for it. When the person in that role leaves or is promoted, they look for a replacement into the exact same role.

Even when businesses have enough foresight to review roles when an employee leaves or is promoted, they still define the role tightly before advertising and hiring.

There are a couple of things that make this traditional approach problematic. Firstly, there's a chance that the existing role holds some level of gender bias. If you're explicitly stating you need someone who is flexible around working longer hours, you're preventing people with caring responsibilities from applying.

There are obviously elements of the job role that will need to be clearly and strictly defined. If you're hiring for a Head of Sales, some managerial experience and sales experience will be necessary to perform the role. Keeping your non-negotiables in the job description is helpful but try not to include the 'nice to have' elements in the job role that you advertise. We've already seen that women will only apply if they meet 100% of the criteria. Having too many 'nice to haves' will cause many women to avoid applying even if they are completely qualified for the role.

For example, if your Head of Marketing left to work for a competitor, instead of dusting off their job description, making cursory changes and posting a job ad, you'd think about the actual outcomes you need from this role. Not the minutiae of the duties but the outcomes and the skills needed to achieve them.

By hiring the right person and then developing the role to leverage the person's strengths and talents, you'll get the best out of your new employee and open up a world of possibilities for the business.

Career Development Support
Hiring more women should be just the start of the process. Companies can do more to nurture women's careers by implementing programs for all employees designed to encourage more diversity in leadership roles.

By investing in hiring, mentoring, sponsorship, and career development, businesses can help ensure that women can attain and retain demanding positions. For businesses willing to commit to this, they will be laying the foundations for a serious competitive advantage in the long term.

Sponsorship
We discussed sponsorship earlier, from the point of view of a woman seeking out a sponsor to champion them. From the other side, women and people at a senior level can look out for suitable women to sponsor.

By implementing an official sponsorship program, you can identify your top talent and pair them with a sponsor to ensure that there is somebody at a high level championing them. By making the sponsorship official, it becomes a transparent process that can be evaluated to make sure it's promoting diversity as intended.

Mentorship
Lots of businesses already have mentorship programs but they are a great way to support and nurture employee development. They're particularly useful when beginning a

new role, to help coach and support.

If you're a very small business, you can connect employees with mentors in similar roles outside of your business. Your local chamber of commerce may even be able to help.

Career Counseling
Career counseling involves making sure that everyone is aware of the career paths open to them. By having regular and open conversations with employees about their ambitions, and the skills and qualifications needed to progress to the next step, you can keep them motivated and engaged.

It also ensures that your talented but more introverted employees don't fall by the wayside simply because they don't aggressively seek out opportunity.

These conversations should be incorporated into regular performance reviews so that conversations about promotions and career progression are specifically linked to employee performance.

Reward Performance Fairly
Reward and recognition schemes can often favor men. Although it's usually an unconscious bias, it's a pervasive one. Examples of schemes that unfairly penalize or restrict women are:
- Only offering bonuses in male-dominated departments, like sales departments.
- Rewarding performance linked with working longer hours, like sheer volume rather than the quality of work. If volume is a key metric, any additional hours worked should be taken into consideration and a production rate per hour might be more appropriate.

- Schemes that reward length of service. Women are more likely to experience a break in employment because of their caring responsibilities.
- Bonuses offered without a clear and transparent framework. For example, a discretionary bonus given by managers without very clear criteria to assess employees against. Studies have shown that even when male and female employees achieve the same goals, the male employee's achievement is often viewed as more impressive.
- Schemes that penalize part-time workers, who are usually women.

Small Businesses Can Lead The Way
Small business owners may feel that the diversity issue isn't one that applies as heavily to them. Small businesses don't have as many employees, and for very small businesses who only employ a few employees, the small numbers can mean that it's almost impossible to achieve a % quota of female leaders.

However, diversity is about a lot more than quotas. For large businesses quotas can be one way that they can have an easy way to identify to measure how they're doing. In a small business, you don't need to do that but you still stand to gain a lot from having a diverse workforce.

Small businesses have a real opportunity to level the playing field. By their nature, smaller businesses are more agile and can make changes quickly without the bureaucratic red tape that plagues multi-national organizations.

Smaller businesses can quickly implement initiatives like creating partnerships with local schools to offer work experience programs to students. And, with a shorter chain of command, filtering cultural change down through the ranks and leading by example is also easier.

The challenges smaller businesses might face is that they may recruit and promote less often, meaning that any changes to their processes could take additional time to be reflected in their leadership team.

However, smaller businesses can lay the foundations for a diverse future by starting to implement changes now so that they can reap the rewards later.

Real Life Case Study – How IBM Encourages Gender Diversity

IBM takes diversity very seriously, with diversity initiatives that go way beyond gender diversity and include various minority groups. Let's take a look at some of their initiatives that focus on gender diversity.

Headed by a female CEO, you could argue that IBM has a head start but they recognize that encouraging diversity is an ongoing and necessary task. Having female leaders isn't 'the end' of a real diversity initiative.

Their diversity programs are particularly effective because they consider diversity as an essential part of their business success, alongside innovation. They embrace diversity as a key differentiator between themselves and their competition and leverage the creative advantage that creates.

IBM runs several programs to attract females to a career in

the IT industry. One of these programs is the Girls Schools' Outreach Program, which was established in 2008 by the UK Women's Leadership Council. The program connects girls aged 15-16 with mentors from IBM and provides work experience for over a hundred female students each year.

IBM also redesigned the career section of its website to provide interviews with senior female leaders and offer specific female-oriented advice about seeking a career at IBM.

They applied flexible working across the board to every job at every level, including job sharing, home working and reduced hours, and working a compressed week. To add to their family-friendly policies, they also provide access to emergency childcare and eldercare providers for employees who might need this temporary support.

For employees on maternity leave, they operate an online community where women can stay connected and find a 'buddy' to support them when they return to work. Fathers are also connected with help, advice, and support in a similar manner.

They also operate a reverse mentoring program, where employees from minority groups share experiences with senior leaders. This keeps the senior leaders in touch with the experiences of lower-level employees and gives those employees direct access to senior leadership.

In recognition of their gender diversity initiatives, IBM was awarded the prestigious Catalyst award in 2018.

So far, in this book, we've focused mostly on women in

established organizations and how they can climb the corporate ladder. However, not all female leaders are taking the more conventional approach. A growing number of women are taking the plunge into entrepreneurship.

In the next chapter, we'll investigate how women are taking the lead by starting their own businesses and creating big change.

Chapter 8 – The Rise and Rise of the Female Entrepreneur

"There is no better personal development tool than running your own business."
Ali Brown, Entrepreneurial Guru for Women.

How Women Are Leveraging Their Strengths In Entrepreneurial Endeavors

When we think of entrepreneurs, most people think of one of the many successful male entrepreneurs like Jeff Bezos, Mark Zuckerberg, or Tim Ferriss.

For a long time, entrepreneurship was a male-dominated territory. The average entrepreneur is in their thirties, at which time a lot of women are busy raising children whilst also potentially working to contribute to household finances. Given that becoming an entrepreneur can involve very long hours and unpredictable income, leaping into entrepreneurship might not even be on women's radar at that time.

However, with the rise of online technology and a surge of interest in gender equality, we're seeing more and more female entrepreneurs. According to the National Association of Women Business Owners, there are over 9 million U.S companies owned by women. These women-owned companies employ over 7 million people and generate approximately $1.5 billion in sales.

Over the last several years there's been a rise in the number of women choosing to set up their own businesses to give them the income and flexibility they need. It's even brought the term 'Mompreneur' into common usage.

So, what's driving more and more women to entrepreneurship? Issues like the ones we've discussed in earlier chapters, like lack of flexible working options and pay disparity have prompted many women to take matters into their own hands. What better way to tackle the issue than to create your own ideal working conditions?

However is entrepreneurship the best way for women to lead the way for positive change?

Female Entrepreneurs Work Differently
In the same way that female leaders, in general, have a different leadership approach than most of their male colleagues, female entrepreneurs do things differently.

On the whole, female entrepreneurs have less ambitious growth aspirations and hire fewer people. This has, in the past, led people to believe that women entrepreneurs were less serious, committed or successful.

Yet that's not the whole picture. A Dow Jones study into U.S venture-backed companies uncovered that the successful companies had twice as many women founders or co-founders. Further research from financial institutions has shown that business loans granted to female founders are less risky and result in fewer write-offs. These findings indicate that by and large, women-owned businesses are more stable and secure.

Women are also more likely to start charitable ventures or businesses with a social/ethical slant to them. There's even a term among some entrepreneurs who consider themselves 'heart-centered'. This means that they run businesses who aren't just about profit – they're about giving something back in some way. Most people who identify as heart-centered entrepreneurs are women.

High Profile Women Entrepreneurs & The Lessons We Can Take

There's some evidence to suggest that female entrepreneurs don't have goals as aggressive as their male counterparts. However, that doesn't mean there aren't plenty of highly successful female entrepreneurs.

Let's take a look at some of the female entrepreneurs who've broken the mold and found great success in many areas, from fashion to health.

Jo Malone: Jo Malone London, Jo Loves
Jo Malone is a UK entrepreneur who founded a global brand, *Jo Malone London*, in 1994 along with her mother, Eileen. She later sold it in 2006 to *Estee Lauder* for an undisclosed amount supposed to be in the millions. In 2011, she founded a new fragrance company, *Jo Loves*.

Jo grew up in social housing in the Bexley Heath area of Kent, a far cry from the upmarket streets that her stores would eventually grace. Starting her career as a facialist, she quickly discovered that she had a talent for mixing fragrances for her homemade beauty products.

Originally selling and gifting her products to customers of her facialist business, she found that she was getting large amounts of repeat orders. She eventually founded *Jo Malone London* to sell them to a wider audience.

Sophia Amoruso: Nasty Gal, Girlboss Media
Sophia Amoruso started her eBay store Nasty Gal Vintage at age 22. She sourced vintage clothing and other items, mostly from thrift stores and resold them at a profit on her eBay store.

In 2008, Sophia left eBay and launched her Nasty Gal retail website.

Amoruso developed a big social media following, which helped propel Nasty Gal on to further success. In 2016 she was listed in Forbes as one of the richest self-made women in the world.
In 2014, she published her autobiography *#GIRLBOSS*, which was later adapted into a Netflix show, Girlboss.

Unfortunately, Nasty Gal ended up filing for bankruptcy shortly after Amoruso stepped down as CEO. It was purchased by the Boohoo Group in 2017 for $20 million.

After the sale of Nasty Gal, Amoruso leveraged her experience as a female leader and her autobiography success to launch Girlboss Media. Girlboss describes itself as, *"a community of strong, curious, and ambitious women redefining success on our own terms."*

Anne Wojcicki: 23andMe
Anne Wojcicki co-founded the human genome research company 23andMe with Linda Avey in 2006. The company name is a reference to the 23 pairs of chromosomes found in a normal human cell. In 2008 their test kit was named the Invention of the Year by Time Magazine.

In 2015 the company gained FDA approval for health-related tests, and in 2018 they began collaboration with

GlaxoSmithKline to develop new medicines from the results of their tests.

High-profile female leaderships seems to run in the family, as her sister, Susan Wojcicki, is the CEO of YouTube

Arianna Huffington: The Huffington Post, Thrive Global

Ariana Huffington co-founded The Huffington Post in 2005 and has an estimated net worth of $50 million. AOL purchased The Huffington Post in 2011 for over $300 million, with Ariana Huffington remaining on board as company president.

Her ex-husband Michael was a politician, and Arianna was quite active in political circles, helping her husband campaign and voicing her own political views. In 2003, she ran against Arnold Schwarzenegger for the California governorship but withdrew from campaigning before the election.

In 2016, Huffington stood down as CEO of The Huffington Post to start a new business, Thrive Global which promotes wellbeing.

She's also the internationally bestselling author of books including *Thrive: The Third Metric to Redefining Success and Creating a Life of Well-Being, Wisdom, and Wonder* and *The Sleep Revolution: Transforming Your Life, One Night At A Time*

Jasmine Crowe: BCG, Goodr

Jasmine Crowe launched her first business, Black Celebrity Giving (BCG) in 2011. BCG was created to highlight, celebrate and support black people doing positive things to impact communities.

In 2017, Jasmine founded her second company Goodr. Goodr uses technology to manage surplus food waste from restaurants and distribute it to the people who needed it most. Goodr allows businesses to register the donations as tax-deductible charity donations – allowing both the business and the recipients to benefit.

Sara Blakely: SPANX
Sarah Blakely came up with the idea for Spanx while working in a sales role for an office supply company. She was inspired by the way the control-top hosiery she wore for work gave a smoother figure. She wanted to recreate that look with a variety of clothing without the need for wearing full hosiery.

She spent two years and all of her $5,000 life savings developing the product. Initially, her product was rejected by hosiery mills, which Blakely noted were mostly owned and run by men who had no experience of being an end-user. Eventually, one of the male owners was encouraged by his daughters to support Blakely's product and a prototype was eventually created.

When Spanx was named one of Oprah Winfrey's Favorite Things, the business took off. Since then, Blakely has been featured on numerous 'Top 100' lists, including Time Magazine and Forbes.

In 2006, she launched the Sara Blakely Foundation, a non-profit organization to help support women through education and entrepreneurial training.

Emily Weiss: Glossier
Emily Weiss launched a beauty blog, Into the Gloss late in 2010, while working as an on-set styling assistant for

Vogue. Into the Gloss did so well that she eventually left her job at Vogue to focus on the blog and related ventures.

In 2013, she began approaching venture capitalists to raise funds for expansion into e-commerce. Glossier was launched in October 2014 with just four beauty products. It has since expanded the range to over six product categories, including Glossiwear, a clothing and accessories range. Glossier was valued at $1.2 billion in March 2019.

Industries That Fit Well with Feminine Skills

As you can see, lots of women have found entrepreneurial success by creating products for women to fill a gap in the market, like Sarah Blakely and Emily Weiss.

Alongside some of the more traditional industries that attract women to create their own businesses – beauty salons, boutiques, hairdressers, etc., more and more women are creating businesses in previously male-dominated industries.

Women are starting to more frequently get into areas like disruptive tech. For example, Jasmine Crowe and Goodr, and often these female-led startups are driven as much by social conscience as by profit.

Women, in general, are well-suited to industries like health and wellbeing, education, and retail. Often when asked, women will say they felt almost 'called' to one of the more feminine industries.

It's important to point out that there is no more or less value in any industry. The key ingredient for most successful entrepreneurs is passion. Is it something you feel passionately about and is it something you can create a business from? If so, then it's got great potential regardless of whether it's flattering undergarments or industry-disrupting software that you're developing.

The crucial message is that women are taking charge and building businesses that ignite their passion. Entrepreneurship gives them the opportunity to drive change by creating companies that are female-led and female-friendly at all levels.

Then there's the fact that some of the more feminine skills are valuable in absolutely any industry. Some of the skills that make female entrepreneurs stand out in male-dominated STEM industries are:

- **Great negotiation skills.** The collaborative approach that comes naturally to a lot of women is an asset when it comes to high-level negotiating.
- **Emotional Intelligence.** The emotional intelligence that most women have comes in handy for everything from identifying what will resonate with your target client to how to manage business relationships.
- **Listening skills.** Women tend to make good listeners, and that can help them identify where they need to make changes based on feedback. It can also help them connect with clients, business partners, and potential investors.

There's no single industry that's better for women to start a business in. If you have the drive and passion, there are no limits!

Building an Effective Online Business

It can be daunting to take that leap into entrepreneurship, especially if you don't have a lot of cash to invest in your new endeavor. Network marketing has, for many years, been the most accessible low-entry-cost option for women who need flexibility and the freedom to be their own boss.

However, the online business world is booming, and work from home/be your own boss opportunities are not limited to network marketing. If you love network marketing and you enjoy building a team, then that's still one option. Many network marketing companies are designed to attract women, and they push the 'working stay at home mom' angle.

However, there are almost endless options for people of any gender to start up an online business with little or no outlay. If you have a business idea, you're one step closer to being your own boss.

Many of the most successful entrepreneurs spotted a gap in the market for a product and service and then provided it. However, there's also success to be had by doing something better than everyone else, or by providing an existing service in a new or better way for a certain target market.

If you have your heart set on inventing or producing a product and don't have a big budget, there are even crowdfunding websites like Kickstarter. These allow you to can gauge public interest as well as raise the funds you need.

There are a lot of ways that you can create your own business with little or no budget. Take NastyGal's founder, Sophia Amoruso. She began her business selling vintage clothing on eBay. She'd visit thrift stores, find classic designer items that the store staff had completely undervalued, snap them up, and then sell them on at a higher price.

There are so many options for starting your own business and they don't all involve selling a product. You can market a skill you have as a service. Lots of women enter into online coaching because their feminine skills like listening and communication tend to make them good coaches. Other popular options are freelance writer, editor, web designer, social media manager, or virtual assistant.

For no initial outlay at all, depending on what you choose, you can market your skills on freelancing sites or use social media to spread the word about your services.

If you want to sell a product with little to no outlay, you can dropship. There are even services where you can design T-Shirts and other easily printed items like mugs and cushions. You then sell them via the service, who prints and ships them on demand.

Of course, there are some considerations. You'll need to have command of the skills that you want to charge people for. You'll also need to investigate if you need any kind of indemnity insurance. There may be specific qualifications or regulatory requirements for your business in the countries you want to operate in. None of that is as difficult as it sounds. However, becoming your own boss isn't always easy.

Overcoming the Challenges of Starting your own Business

To run a successful business – whatever your definition of success – you, first of all, need to believe that you can do it. The same lack of confidence that stops women applying for jobs when they don't match the role 100% can stop women from believing they have what it takes to become an entrepreneur.

Even once you believe you can do it, there are practical considerations to factor in. If your business needs funding, you may need to raise venture capital, which can be a long and arduous process.

If you're starting small scale and low budget, you may not need to worry about investors, but you will need to find clients and customers. If you've never needed to do this before it can be very daunting.

Almost all business owners experience periods of financial and emotional difficulty as they navigate the waters of self-employment. You're free of many of the constraints of the formal corporate world but becoming a business owner brings many of its own challenges.

Why The Challenges Of Female Entrepreneurship Are Worth It

Women are increasingly becoming entrepreneurs – and they're increasingly very successful at it. According to one survey by Smallbiztrends.com, over half of female entrepreneurs expected their incomes to increase in 2018. This was on a level with the number of males who also felt their income would increase.

Over the last decade, businesses owned by women have

grown at a 1.5 times greater rate than other small businesses. The tides are beginning to turn in a big way towards female entrepreneurship.

Then there's the flexibility and freedom that comes with being your own boss. While it might not come easily at first, once you've built a client base, you are effectively in complete control. Your income is completely linked to your own performance, and you can work the hours you choose. Even better, your own business never comes with a glass ceiling because you're starting right at the top.

Building A Business That Nurtures And Supports Other Women

The other great thing about becoming your own boss and building a business is that you can nurture and support other women. Your entire business can be built around nurturing and supporting other women by becoming a coach, or by creating products that are designed for women.

Yet any business can support and nurture women by hiring other women, joining networking groups, and offering advice or training to other women.

With female-owned businesses employing over 7 million people in the U.S, their contribution to the economy is impressive. Even better, female entrepreneurs are in the unique position of being able to implement female-friendly working practices from day one.

As many women start businesses in the hope that they will be able to achieve a proper work-life balance, that ethos remains when they are ready to hire their first employees. As such, female entrepreneurs know that women with caring responsibilities are perfectly capable of achieving the same work to the same standard as a male employee.

Even by simply being a female business owner, you're a powerful role model for other women. By recognizing that and aiming to support and inspire other women to achieve the same, female entrepreneurs can make a huge contribution to gender diversity.

There are lots of ways that women can become leaders, right down to taking the matter into their own hands and forming their own businesses. There's lots that we can all do to keep pushing forward and leading the way towards gender diversity.

One of the ways we can make things better for the future is to start to nurture young women and girls early in their educational journey. In the next chapter, we'll look at what can be done to develop the female leaders of tomorrow and make their path a little clearer.

Chapter 9 – Nurturing The Next Generation Of Female Leaders

"I love to see a young girl go out and grab the world by the lapels. Life's a bitch. You've got to go out and kick ass."
Maya Angelou, American poet, singer, memoirist, and civil rights activist.

There's a lot that working women can do to help encourage gender diversity in their workplaces. However, to work against the biases that currently exist we need to start addressing the issues early on.

Starting to prepare young leaders of all genders while they are in high school can help to redefine the next generation's idea of what a great leader looks like. It can even help us remove gender from the equation.

Combatting Gender Bias Fast

"Don't let anyone rob you of your imagination, your creativity, or your curiosity. It's your place in the world; it's your life."
Dr. Mae Jemison, Engineer, physician, and NASA astronaut.

Numerous studies are showing that female students are encouraged down different paths to male students quite early in their education. To combat this, high schools should review their career guidance policies to remove gender biases.

Another factor that can have an impact on how young

people view leadership and gender is the lack of female leaders in high schools. Women are underrepresented across educational leadership in the same way they are underrepresented across the private sector and government.

Girls and young women need to have role models to look to and imagine that they could achieve similar things. With a lack of obvious female leader role models in the school system, it's even more important that the curriculum addresses the topic. How can this be done?

High school is a particularly relevant time to tackle the gender biases that are hidden in the school system. It's well known that adolescence is a difficult time, and it's a time when children begin to really feel the weight of societal gender norms.

As we've discussed earlier, they will have been aware of these norms since pre-school and before. However, they can begin to heavily affect the choices girls make and the aspirations they have during high school.

Several studies have confirmed that the notion of males as assertive and females as passive is reinforced in classrooms. Males will often dominate any discussion in the classroom and volunteer their opinions freely. Female students, on the other hand, tend to be less willing to put themselves forward.

This difference in behavior leads to teachers unconsciously tending to request input from male students more than female ones. This means that girls rarely speak up in class – a behavior that then carries across into other mixed-gender environments and is eventually demonstrated in the workplace as a reluctance to speak up.

After thousands of observation hours in various classrooms and grade levels, the research team behind the book, *Still Failing at Fairness: How Gender Bias Cheats Girls and Boys in School and What We Can Do About It*, found that the amount of gender bias in lessons and teaching practices, in their words was 'startling'. Their study unearthed that teachers asked female students fewer questions than male students and frequently provided males with more feedback.

However, stereotype reinforcement doesn't stop there. The teaching materials used to deliver the curriculum often demonstrate gender bias. Textbook authors are predominantly male, and characterizations in teaching materials are frequently male, and frequently adhere to gender stereotypes.

Several UNESCO studies found that women were underrepresented in numerous texts, and many contain stereotypes or even offensive comments about women.

To eradicate gender bias, the teaching materials used in high schools need to represent genders equally, and not attach stereotypes to them. For example, textbooks should contain strong female role models as well as male ones and describe their achievements in a non-gendered way. When this is the case, we'll be one step closer to raising a generation of people that aren't plagued by unconscious biases.

Changing the content of educational materials will take time and funds that not all schools have access to. Teachers can help speed the process up by identifying and calling out gender biases in their educational materials. They can also ensure that they call on the opinions of their female students as frequently as the male ones.

Mentoring Programs
One way to encourage leadership skills in young women is to connect them with mentors early in their careers. Mentors can even be employed during high school and college to help advise and guide students through the various choices that can impact their future career.

There are existing organizations that mentor girls and young women, often in underprivileged communities where their support is needed the most.

These organizations connect young women with mentors who encourage their ambition, help them set and achieve goals, and boost their confidence. Some are working with specialist industries like STEM subjects, journalism, and tech to encourage more young women to pursue roles in these industries.

Organizations like these are crucial for empowering and inspiring our next generation of female leaders.

Even in locations where these organizations aren't accessible, or for more general mentoring, there are ways that teachers and female leaders in the community can help. We often think of mentoring as a completely 1-1 relationship, and 1-1 is indeed the most common, ideal method.

However, group mentoring is also a valuable resource for young women who may not be able to access other support. With group mentoring, it only takes one champion willing to lead the sessions, and they can invite other female leaders to share their knowledge and experience in sessions. By allowing young women to discuss the challenges and rewards of leadership with a real female leader, they can understand what's possible to achieve in their own lives.

Group mentoring is a very flexible and adaptable way to give young women access to the support they need. Beyond providing role models, mentoring allows young women to start to develop the real-life skills that they'll need to become future leaders.

Skills like communication, negotiation, stakeholder management, and collaboration can all be learned in a mentoring environment. Not only will developing these skills stand young women in good stead for their future careers but it will also boost their self-esteem too.

Real Life Case Study of Mentorship and Support

The Young Women Leaders Program (YWLP) at the University of Virginia has been successfully running for over 20 years. It employs both group mentoring and individual mentoring to encourage young future female leaders.

They have linked with four local area middle schools, who each nominate girls that they believe would benefit from the program. Those girls are then matched with individual mentors from the college as well as allocated a group for weekly two-hour sessions that continue for a year.

As well as their individual mentors attending group sessions with them, once a week, participants meet with

their personal mentor for one-on-one support. The group sessions focus on problem-solving, decision making and developing leadership skills in the girls.
Discussion, prompts and activities help the groups engage with the topics presented.

The program has the added benefit of being located on a university campus, allowing the participants some exposure to this type of environment. For some of the girls, it may be the first time that they've considered attending a college after high school.

The results of the program are impressive. An evaluation revealed that over three-quarters of the participants stated that the program helped them:
- improve the way they listen to people with views different from their own,
- support and talk with their friends,
- deal with their problems,
- communicate with other kids at school,
- interact with people who are different from them,
- think about their future.

Over two-thirds reported that the program helped them improve their self-esteem, get involved in school as a leader, make decisions about their behavior at school, and deal with difficult situations.

Investing in women's leadership, starting in schools, has the power to bring about widespread change. It's not a short-term solution but a commitment to the future. Investing in young women's leadership will not only change the trajectory of their future but that of the entire business world as well.

Conclusion: Be Strong, Lead, Find Success

"How wonderful it is that nobody need wait a single moment before starting to improve the world."
Anne Frank, German diarist.

Despite the differences in male and female leadership styles, both men and women can make incredibly effective leaders. The differences are apparent in various studies but the percentages are small. Additionally, all of the research only demonstrates averages, and there is a vast variance among individuals.

Leadership ability is rarely about the gender of the leader and is more about the individual. However, our innate unconscious gender biases and social expectations can cause us to view male and female leaders differently. It's those biases and societal expectations that need to be addressed so that we can all move forward into a more gender-diverse future.

The burden of changing the way we think about women in leadership falls to all of us. By dispassionately identifying when we're allowing gender bias to influence the way we perceive other people, we can become aware when it is happening and take steps to change our perceptions.

The good news is that change is happening and it's happening at a fast rate. Women's issues are getting more and more media coverage, and fewer women and men are willing to tolerate unfairness in the workplace.

To challenge gender discrimination, there are lots of things you can do. To recap, here are some positive actions that we can all take in the workplace.

Speak Up

"It took me quite a long time to develop a voice, and now that I have it, I am not going to be silent."
Madeleine Albright, Former U.S. Secretary of State.

Share your opinions and your ambitions freely. Showing up and working hard is essential but giving yourself the best chance of moving up the corporate ladder means you'll need to be heard.

Be your own advocate, and seek out a sponsor who can also speak up on your behalf. Make it clear to your managers and colleagues exactly what you bring to the table and why it's valuable.

Keep Learning
Invest in learning how to be the best at your role. Back up your opinions with facts and data when possible to lend your arguments extra credibility. Take an interest in the overall business goals and strategy and figure out how your ambitions align with the company.

Keep in touch with developments in your industry, and have conversations with your colleagues and superiors about them. Doing this demonstrates your commitment to the organization's success, as well as showing that you have the commercial knowledge and understanding to make significant leadership decisions that take the broader context into account. In short, work towards making yourself an invaluable expert!

Seek Out Mentors And Sponsors
Mentors and sponsors have different roles to play in your career progression but they're both incredibly valuable.

Take advantage of any programs in your workplace designed to link you with a mentor or a sponsor.

If your workplace doesn't have a program, seek them out yourself. Mentors can even be external to your organization. Any mentor should have experience and knowledge that would be directly relevant to your role or the role that you consider to be your next step.

Recognize Your Achievements And Strengths
Don't allow perfectionism or self-confidence issues to hold you back. Keep a note of your achievements and celebrate them. From academic certifications to landing a new client for your organization, make sure that you recognize the value and knowledge that you have.

Take chances and put yourself out there. Apply for a role you want even if you don't meet 100% of the criteria. When you see an opportunity, take it.

Embrace Your Femininity
Allow yourself to express your opinions and handle situations in a way that makes the best use of your strengths. When those strengths are traits that are perceived as feminine, embrace that. Don't try to fit a mold made for somebody else.

Don't try too hard to emulate more masculine traits if those don't come naturally. Forcing yourself to behave in a way that's not natural simply to appear more like 'leadership material' can make you feel miserable and can also have the opposite effect.

You're already leadership material. Anyone can learn the skills it takes to be a leader but to do it well, you need to work with your natural personality traits. By trying to force masculine behaviors, you're reinforcing the message to yourself and to everyone else that only masculine traits are leadership traits.

Instead of the 'if you can't beat them join them' approach, remember that you're a role model for other aspiring leaders. Demonstrate to them – and yourself – that women are already competent and effective leaders.

With continued perseverance, we can all contribute to the movement towards gender equality. The ultimate goal is to live and work in a world where men and women are honestly considered equal in their social roles.

To get there, we need to work together, to challenge outdated gender stereotypes that currently hold so many people back. Now go out there and change the world!

"If the first woman God ever made was strong enough to turn the world upside down all alone, these women together ought to be able to turn it back, and get it right side up again! And now they is asking to do it, the men better let them."
Sojourner Truth, American abolitionist.

Confidence & Assertive Skills for Women.

How to become a Strong, Independent, Confident Woman in the Modern World.

Angelina Williams

Copyright © Angelina Williams Publishing

All rights reserved.
No part of this publication may be reproduced, distributed, or transmitted in any form or by any means, including photocopying, recording, or other electronic or mechanical methods, without the prior written permission of the publisher, except in the case of brief quotations embodied in critical reviews and certain other non-commercial uses permitted by copyright law.

Introduction: Have The Confidence To Be A Strong, Calm Woman in the Modern World

When was the last time you stood up for yourself? I mean, *really* stood up for yourself, put forward your needs, wants and opinions, and had other people listen to you? Let me guess; it was a while ago, if ever, and you had to psyche yourself up first.

Think about all those times that you *wish* you'd been assertive enough to speak your mind and how much you want to be able to do it right now. To say 'no' to your demanding boss who drops a pile of work on your desk at the end of the day; to tell your coworker that you won't take on her share of the latest project this time; to let your husband know that you need more help with the kids. Or to finally take back that product that hasn't worked since you bought it, rather than consigning it to the appliance graveyard in the basement.

I'm guessing that if you've picked up this book, the letting things slide by far outweighs the standing up for yourself. Am I right? If only confidence came naturally. If only assertiveness could be bought at your local 7-11!

I'm not going to lie to you; nothing comes that easily, even if it *looks* like it for some (and trust me, a lot of those so-called self-assured people are 'faking it 'til they make it'). There is some good news, however: confidence can be worked on and improved. In fact, it's rather like a muscle; the more you use it, the stronger it becomes. Heck, yes!

Assertiveness too is a learned skill. You can LEARN to be assertive and to stand up for yourself without feeling like you want to throw up at the same time. Double yes!

This book is chock full of tips and strategies to help you become a more confident and assertive woman. You will learn to recognize your default communication style, understand the difference between them all and also where you might need to change or improve.

We'll also consider the traditional reasons for a lack of confidence – a problem that unfairly plagues many women – and then look at how you can address it. I'll offer strategies for the mind and soul, including developing a positive mindset and how to develop mental toughness. You will be given encouragement to play to your feminine strengths: yes we usually are more emotionally intelligent than men, show you how to act 'as if', discuss EFT and use visualization to silence your inner critic as well as build confidence. A lot of this will involve taking risks and finding the courage to help to improve it further but don't worry, I will walk you through all of that.

Throughout, I'll give you specific strategies to do all of the above. We'll also talk about the issue of assertiveness in different contexts – such as at work, with your team, in interviews, at home with loved ones and friends, and during moments of awkwardness such as receiving or giving criticism and more.

I've also got some great tips on strong communication for assertive women and lots of inspiration from other women in here too!
Indeed, this book is peppered throughout with inspirational stories of ordinary women just like *yourself* doing amazing

things. From the women behind the phenomenal #MeToo movement to Nobel Laureates to ordinary women doing extraordinary things, I'll showcase their story here.

If they can do it, so can you!

Don't believe me?

Why? Is it you think these women must have something extra special to achieve their success? Confidence in spades, or inbuilt natural charisma? Not true. Many of these women are beset by insecurities and fears at times too, just like you.

- From the Nobel laureate who worries about being 'found out,
- To the award-winning actress attending Harvard who secretly frets about being dumb,
- To the superstar singing sensation who still sometimes feels like the 'loser kid' back at school,
- To women leaders and manager who admit to self-doubt,
- All the way to Presidential hopefuls and female senators who struggle to make themselves heard.

All of these women face many of the same confidence issues as you; the difference is that they haven't let it stop them… and you won't either after reading this book.

They're all great women to take inspiration from. And if you ever doubt the difference that assertive women can make, you need to look no further than the phenomenal #MeToo and Time's Up movements…

It's Time For Massive Positive Change

As I write this, we're nearing March 8 – International Women's Day. Let's hope that this year is as influential a year for women as previous years were, thanks to the groundbreaking *#MeToo* movement.

"The high road for a woman for centuries was silence. The new high road is speaking up."
Zoe Saldana

The *#MeToo* movement was first started by activist Tarana Burke in 2007 but captured the attention of the world 10 years later, following allegations of sexual assault against Hollywood's Harvey Weinstein.

Actress Alyssa Milano tweeted to her followers that anyone who experienced sexual abuse or harassment should reply *#MeToo* to show the scale of the problem. And boy, did they do just that, with 66,000 users replying directly to Milano that same day.

It didn't stop there. In the following year (Oct 2017–Oct 2018), the *#MeToo* hashtag was used more than 19 MILLION times on Twitter… working out to an average of 55,319 uses A DAY, says the Pew Research Center. There were also millions of mentions on Instagram, Facebook and other social media platforms around the world.
Other similar campaigns – such as *#BalanceTonPorc, #YoTambien, #QuellaVoltaChe, #NotYourHabibti* (in the Palestinian territories), **#NiUnaMenos** – took off in Italy, Spain, Japan, Argentina, Australia, China, France, South Korea, Sweden and more.

Other hashtag movements were also set up to combat sexual harassment in the wake of *#MeToo*, such as

#AidToo (humanitarian aid sector), *#Tekniskfel* (Sweden's tech industry), and *#MosqueMeToo* (created by Muslim women highlighting sexual abuse during the annual pilgrimage to Mecca.)

TIME magazine named the *#MeToo* cause and all the women involved as its 2017 Person of the Year.

Sample Stories

Morgana McKenzie was a young camera operator harassed by a colleague. He would yell at her and rip the camera off her shoulders daily. The harassment turned physical after he forced himself on her one day when giving her a ride home from set.
USA Today

Being raped once made it easier to be raped again. I instinctually shut down. My body remembered, so it protected me.
I disappeared. #metoo
Because I was shamed and considered a "party girl" I felt I deserved it. I shouldn't have been there, I shouldn't have been "bad" #metoo
American actress, model and musician, @evanrachelwood

#MeToo – Crowded tram at Disney, sat a row behind my family. Man kept his hand on my thigh the whole ride, stroking the fine hair there. His friend looked on. Think I was 11 but scared to confirm dates of that trip with my mom, because I never told anyone. Us too. All of us.
American actress, @Allison_Tolman

#MeToo - I had a cardiologist – who was my employer – trap me inside an office, locked the door, and whipped his penis out for me to touch it. Paralyzed initially, I knew I had to get out of the room because I was the only person in the entire building. I became angry, demanded that he unlock the door, and then I threatened him that he would lose his medical license... he thought that he could slip me a $100 bill to keep my mouth shut.
Lynette Janine

I've lost count of how many times I've lied and told a guy I have a boyfriend because he wouldn't take a simple "no" for an answer #MeToo
@thesaraharley

Every single woman who wrote *#MeToo* displayed incredible courage and bravery – I have tips on finding your own courage later in the book.

It's fair to say the response to *#MeToo* was unprecedented. Somehow millions of women around the globe found the confidence – from each other, from the movement and from deep within themselves – to speak up and speak out.

I remember the sheer inspirational power of turning on my Facebook feed and seeing the words *#MeToo* written by friends, colleagues and acquaintances, many of whom were speaking out for the first time.

Did you know that traditionally three out of four women who experience workplace harassment never report it to anyone in power, so says the U.S. Equal Employment Opportunities Commission. I have tips on how to deal with sexual harassment in the workplace later in this book if this is something personal to you too.

Consequences

In the year since *#MeToo*, 425 prominent people across a range of industries have been publicly accused of sexual misconduct, according to Bloomberg. Everything from serial rape to abuse of power and lewd comments. Together they face 1,700 separate claims of misconduct and harassment.

Hundreds of accused men have been forced to retire, and in the U.S., there are at least 29 new bills passed or pending to protect against sexual harassment at the state level.

Time's Up, started by more than 300 women in Hollywood, is a wider movement than *#MeToo*, intended to tackle all forms of workplace inequality. You may have seen actors and actresses dressed in black and wearing Time's Up pins at the Golden Globes. It's Legal Defense Fund director Sharyn Tejani says the organization has received 3,500 referrals from employees.

Because, of course, sexual harassment and workplace inequality aren't just restricted to the casting couch. Women from all spheres of life – academics, librarians, classical musicians, fast food workers, retail employees and more – have spoken out and demanded change. Their stories have been covered by local media, trade publications, blogs, college newspapers, Twitter and more.

This book, of course, is not about sexual abuse or harassment per se, but I mention the *#MeToo* movement because it's a great example of women-power. It's all about confidence… women across the globe finding the confidence to stand up and say, *'enough is enough'*. Being assertive enough to find the strength to share their stories to empower others.

We can learn from that strength. We can find it within ourselves to be strong, confident and assertive women – to be our best selves.
And it starts right here, right now.

Read on for Chapter 1 – all about the confidence gap and defining just what we mean when we talk about assertiveness...

Chapter 1 – Defining Terms For The Future

Real Life Case Study – Rebecca

Rebecca, a close friend of mine, is one of the most inspiring women I know. She seems to have an unending supply of energy, enthusiasm, and talent, as well as a terrifyingly efficient work ethic that puts mine to shame.

A travel writer, known internationally for her reportage style, she has been published – regularly – in the likes of Marie Claire, The New York Times, Washington Post, TIME, The Guardian, Cosmopolitan and many more. She's also written a couple of books.

In short, she's pretty amazing. She seeks new challenges, while the rest of us search for the perfect pair of jeans but here's one thing you would never guess about her – she's sometimes hamstrung by (an undeserved) lack of confidence.

"I've achieved more than I thought I ever would with my career," admits Rebecca, *"but I still keep expecting someone to say, 'hold on, you don't deserve this' or for the calls from commissioning editors to dry up one day.*

"Part of me thinks I got into this career through luck – just being in the right place at the right time – and I wonder if I've coasted on the back of that ever since."

She hasn't, of course, and thankfully, Rebecca recognizes this for what it is – a classic sign of the *confidence gap* that plagues many women. The fact that she feels it at all, however, is a testament to how pervasive the confidence gap can be.

And she's not alone.

Imposter Syndrome

All too often women who seemingly have it all on the surface lack confidence underneath. Why do so many of us, no matter how talented, skilled or intelligent, struggle with their self-worth?

They are crippled by doubt, feeling imposters in their own lives, worried that someone somewhere will realize they don't deserve to be a mother, a teacher, an actress, a writer, a doctor or a manager [insert your own ambition here].

Men don't seem to have such worries, or if they do, they don't let it stop them… hence the term.

The *confidence gap* between men and women separates the genders.

And it affects women of all ages and careers, even women in power or female role models. Take, for example, these quotes:

"The beauty of the impostor syndrome is you vacillate between extreme egomania, and a complete feeling of: 'I'm a fraud! Oh god, they're on to me! I'm a fraud!' So, you just try to ride the egomania when it comes and enjoy it, and then slide through the idea of fraud."
Hollywood comedian, actress and author, Tina Fey

*"I have written 11 books, but each time I think, 'uh oh, they're going to find out now. I've run a game on

everybody, and they're going to find me out.'"
Civil rights activist, author, poet and Nobel Laureate, Maya Angelou

"The greatest obstacle for me has been the voice in my head that I call my obnoxious roommate. I wish someone would invent a tape recorder that we could attach to our brains to record everything we tell ourselves. We would realize how important it is to stop this negative self-talk."
Co-founder of The Huffington Post, Arianna Huffington

"I still sometimes feel like a loser kid in high school and I just have to pick myself up and tell myself that I'm a superstar every morning so that I can get through this day and be for my fans what they need for me to be."
Singer, songwriter, actress, Oscar winner, Lady Gaga

"Today, I feel much like I did when I came to Harvard Yard as a freshman in 1999. I felt like there had been some mistake, that I wasn't smart enough to be in this company, and that every time I opened my mouth, I would have to prove that I wasn't just a dumb actress."
Academy Award-winning actress Natalie Portman

"I have spent my years since Princeton, while at law school and in my various professional jobs, not feeling completely a part of the worlds I inhabit. I am always looking over my shoulder wondering if I measure up."
The U.S.'s first Hispanic Supreme Court Justice, Sonia Sotomayor

"Every time I took a test, I was sure that it had gone badly. And every time I didn't embarrass myself -- or even excelled -- I believed that I had fooled everyone yet again. One day soon, the jig would be up."
Facebook COO and founder of Leanin.org, Sheryl Sandberg

"There are still days when I wake up feeling like a fraud, not sure I should be where I am."
Sheryl Sandberg

When researching their book *Womenomics*, authors Katty Kay and Claire Shipman kept *"bumping up against a dark spot that we couldn't identify, a force clearly holding them [women] back."*
They said, *"Why did the successful investment banker mention to us that she didn't really deserve the big promotion she'd just got? What did it mean when the engineer who'd been a pioneer in her industry for decades told us offhandedly that she wasn't sure she was really the best choice to run her firm's new big project?"*

Answer: it's all because of the confidence gap. I've seen many women of my acquaintance struggle with it and I haven't been totally immune from it either.

There have been times, a couple in my career, when I've landed jobs that I didn't think I had a hope of getting. I mean, these were big, dream jobs, and in my less confident moments, I was positive I didn't have the experience, or the skills, needed to do them.

Luckily, I refused to listen to my internal naysayer and

applied for them anyway. And trust me, great things can happen when you do that.

The first time I ever had to stand up in front of my five-strong team and lead the morning meeting was nerve-wracking and I'm sure my voice broke several times. But I got through it. The second day wasn't as bad, and a week later, I realized I felt like an old-hat at it. Who would have thought?!

And I will never forget the first time I had to stand up in front of the entire company of, oh just 120 people or so, and give my first solo presentation. My butterflies were having butterflies.
My inner coward shouted, *'I can't do this!'* but I forced myself to do it anyway. Being a shy child, I long ago learned the art of acting *'as if'*, of forcing yourself to do something that other people possibly wouldn't think twice about. I recommend it; it's good for the soul, and as it turns out, good for your building confidence too.

But short of being uncomfortable to deal with, does it really make a difference if we women lack confidence? Oh, heck yes!

Consequences Of The Confidence Gap

Studies show that while your competence may get your foot in the door, it's your confidence – in your work, your performance and yourself – that helps you to get ahead. In short, success is as closely aligned with *confidence* as it is with *competence*.

Which is why a woman's lack of confidence can hold her back from success. It goes some way to explaining why gender inequality at work is still such a big problem.

I mean, we've come far in recent decades, haven't we? In the United States, for instance, more women than men gain graduate degrees. In the UK, the picture is the same. Men are less likely to go to university and are more likely to drop out if they do; likewise, women tend to gain better degrees with higher qualifications than men.

And yet, once we enter the working world, we women are still *paid less* while *men are promoted more*. So, what gives?

The Statistics

A 2018 Women In Management study by Catalyst reports that women only hold just under 24% of senior management roles across the globe, and that figure is falling. (It was 25% in 2017).
Women account for just 22% of senior roles in business in the UK, and while we account for almost half of the workforce in the U.S. (46.9%), only 39.8% of us made manager level in 2017.

As Catalyst concludes about the United States: **"There are fewer women in leadership positions than there are men named John."**

So, what happens between university where women excel, and working life where women are still failing to shatter the glass ceiling? Why are the boardroom doors still closed to so many of us?

It's true that motherhood and children can change our priorities; many women voluntarily take a step away from the working world to have and raise children. There are also institutional reasons and barriers to success that women have been banging their heads against for decades. We'll talk about these in further detail in chapter four.

But we can't get away from one fundamental fact – *women's lack of confidence is also to blame for limiting our own success.*

In 2011, for instance, the UK Institute of Leadership and Management (ILM) surveyed British managers about their confidence at work. HALF of women managers admitted having self-doubts about their job performance or careers. In contrast, only 31% of men admitted the same.

This lack of confidence can impact a woman's entire career trajectory. The same report discovers that women are less likely to apply for promotions and tend to have lower career aspirations than men because of it.

Did you know:

- Men ask for salary raises four times more often than women do.
- When women do negotiate, they ask for 30% less money than men.
- Studies show women underestimate their abilities and performance, while men overestimate both of theirs. In reality, both perform the same.
- According to an internal Hewlett Packard report, women only apply for promotion when they are confident that they meet 100% of the requirements/qualifications. Men tend to apply when they meet 60%.

Even young women under 30 today – despite years of talk about workplace inequality and feminism – have fewer career ambitions than their male counterparts. In the ILM survey, only 30% of young women expect to become managers in their lifetime, compared to 45% of men.

The ILM report concludes: *"The research reveals that women managers are impeded in their careers by lower ambitions and expectations. Compared to their male counterparts, they tend to lack self-belief and confidence – which leads to a cautious approach to career opportunities – and follow a less straightforward career path. The higher expectations and increased confidence of male managers propel them into management roles on average three years earlier than women.*

"We also found that women with low confidence have lower expectations of reaching a leadership and management role and are actually less likely to achieve their career ambitions."

In short, we are standing in the way of our own success.

Are You Your Own Worst Enemy?

Take the case of a male manager in my company. He had a vacancy he wanted to fill internally and had narrowed it down to two people in his team – a woman and a man.

This manager freely confessed over lunch that the woman was more qualified, would do a superior job on paper and probably deserved the role. And then he went ahead and promoted the man.

Now I have no doubt this manager believed in equal pay, rights, and equality for women. He was a good friend of mine and I felt I could speak freely with him *(ok, so after I ranted at him for 10 minutes)*, I asked him why he'd promoted the less qualified male candidate.

He replied honestly, that while he wanted to promote the woman, the man gained more attention throughout the company, thus promoting his department better. He spoke up in meetings, he brought in suggestions for improvements without being asked, and he outright asked for the job, demonstrating ambition. The woman? She did none of those things, and it was harder for others to believe in her competency as a result.

As much as I hated to admit it, as a fellow manager, I understood his logic. It was yet another example of how women can be their own worst enemies when it comes to achieving success.

Of course, I should issue a caveat here – something to demonstrate that I'm not naïve or solely blaming women. Gender bias is very real, and a woman who is confident and assertive in the workplace is likely to be treated very differently to a man who acts the same. Trust me, I've experienced it first-hand. It's a hard lesson to learn, but unfortunately, that's living in the real world at present.

I plan to talk more about the gender bias backlash in chapter four. We'll also talk more about the numerous theories suggested for the confidence gap – anything from the female habit of assuming the blame when things go wrong but crediting others when they go right; to suffering from perfectionism; to nature and nurture combined.

For now though, what's our takeaway from this?

That unless we consider ourselves perfect, we shouldn't volunteer, put ourselves forward or *'lean in'*? But hang on, men have no such qualms!

Don't men ever have doubts? Of course, they do. They are human too *(most of them, anyway)*. But here's the thing – they don't let that stop them. If anything, men tend towards overconfidence.

So why do we hamper ourselves in such a way?

As women, we need to realize that it's not enough to keep our heads down and hope our talent and skills will be recognized. We need to step up, step forward and let our confidence shine.

The good news is that confidence is like a muscle, it can be worked on and strengthened with everyday use. As can assertiveness. And here's the great thing about doing so – it creates a virtuous circle.

More confidence => More assertiveness => Action => Success => More confidence…

By thinking less and acting more, we train our brains to be ready for action rather than passivity.

For future success rather than a self-enforced plateau of achievement.

So, listen up. We're not imposters. We're not inferior.

We deserve success and we deserve to be confident in ourselves, our lives and our jobs. So, let's get out of our own way, and make that happen.

Let's use that confidence muscle and learn how to be assertive… read on.

What Do We Mean By Assertiveness?

I've mentioned this word – assertive – quite a lot in this book already, but what exactly do I mean by that? Ask five different people and they'll probably each give you a conflicting answer.

Is it simply standing up for yourself and your rights? Does it matter what other people want? If people don't listen, is it ok to shout?

Real Life Case Study – Trinity

Trinity, now 35, had a kick-ass mentor during her early career; this was a woman respected by many, disliked by some, but always listened to. Trinity's Mentor had tried to mold Trinity in her image and all was going well until one day, her mentor just quit and left Trinity to her own devices.

"I tried to put what I'd learned into practice without her," says Trinity. *"After an initial wobble, I found my feet. I felt strong, in charge, and pretty kick-ass myself. But things weren't quite right. I started to have more conflicts with opposing departments in meetings and less agreement; people were getting angry around me, including me too sometimes. I was still in charge, but it seemed harder and harder to get things done."*

She recalls, *"I used to come home from work exhausted, wondering why the rest of the company wouldn't work harmoniously with me. In my most paranoid moments, I'd actually wonder, were they really all out to just get me?"*

The answer came during a surprise company away day for bonding.

"We were split into small groups to role play. I was paired with another woman in our company, older than me by 10 years, a manager herself. I liked her, but she was advertising (all about the money!) while I was editorial (about the ethics!). To that point, we'd never played well together in that company, as both sides fought for the upper hand.

"We started our role play and it soon became fraught. And then she said something to me that I've never forgotten to this day. Putting her shields down, she said, 'it must be really hard for you. Your mentor has gone, and you're left trying to be her. But you know, you don't really have to do things the same way that she did. It's ok to work with other people sometimes, to stand your ground when you need to but to negotiate the rest of the time. You don't need to be aggressive to be assertive.'"

Trinity shakes her head at the recollection. *"I kid you not, that was the first time that I realized how aggressive I was being. In my desperation to maintain what my mentor had built (through blood, sweat, tears and the occasional raised voice), I had taken my bid to be assertive too far... and moved into aggression."*

It's an easy mistake to make, and a fine line that many people struggle with. But assertiveness is not aggression. Nor should it be.

As **Psycholgy.com** defines it, assertiveness is, *"being able to stand up for your own rights, communicating your wants, needs, positions and boundaries in a calm and clear manner while respecting other people's thoughts and wishes."*

Trinity had been doing the former, not necessarily the latter, and not always in a calm manner either.

What Does Real Assertiveness Look Like?

Think of assertiveness as the middle ground between aggression and passivity.

- You **CAN** be assertive without being rude or aggressive
- You **CAN** defend your views while still being open to constructive criticism
- You **CAN** be assertive and still tactful and respectful
- You **CAN** be assertive while still recognizing that people's basic human rights (your own and other people's) should be upheld.

Let's talk about that last one for a moment. Everyone has human rights that should be respected and upheld, including you. These rights include being able to express opinions and feelings; being able to make decisions, or even change them; to say no without guilt; to say 'I don't know/ understand'; to have personal freedom; to have privacy.

- If you don't say anything – i.e., react **passively** – your own human rights may be ignored, neglected or trampled upon.
- If you react **aggressively**, however, you may be disrespecting other people's human rights not to be shouted at/intimidated.
- The solution is to act **assertively,** to protect your own rights while not trampling on, or dismissing, anyone else's.

Always remember that people have the right to disagree with you; they have the right to say no.

So, if you tend to make your point while interrupting and talking over others, invading someone's personal space, or put yourself and your needs ahead of them and theirs, I would look again at your communication style. You could be too aggressive.

Of course, that's most often not the problem, is it? And if you've picked up this book, chances are you struggle to be *assertive enough*. Assertiveness is directly linked with confidence, so if you're lacking in the latter, you're going to struggle with the former.

The good news is that all of the strategies to boost your confidence throughout this book will also help your assertiveness, and vice versa.

Women's' Context Conscious Problem

Let me tell you something fundamental before we go any further: The notion that women can't be as assertive as men is a big fat MYTH.

While a study by the Gender Action Portal at Harvard Kennedy School did demonstrate that men tend to exhibit assertive behavior more often than women, they point out that it's not because the women are incapable of it. Indeed, women have the same abilities as men to be assertive BUT they are, what the portal defines as, 'context conscious'.

What the heck does that mean?

It goes back to what I touched on briefly earlier in this chapter, and what I'll talk about in much more detail in chapter four… how we as women are perceived when we are assertive or negotiate on our own behalf.

You see, studies show that women negotiate another person's salary much more effectively – and assertively – than they do their own. That's not true of men.

So, it's not that we lack skills, we just choose *when* to assert them. But why are we so reticent to negotiate our own salaries? What is stopping us from going after our own pay rises, needs and wants just as assertively as we negotiate on behalf of others?

It all boils down to this: **societies' stereotyping of women**.

As much as we might wish that we live in a truly equal society, as far as we've come in recent decades, even as much as we might want to argue that we're just as strong as men in a man's world... we're still judged for our 'female' choices and behavior.

Negotiation, of course, is not intrinsically male or female, masculine or feminine. But from early childhood, girls are taught to be 'nice', to behave, to listen to others. Boys, well, they're expected to be all rough and tumble, loud and rambunctious, because *boys will be boys.*
As we grow up, men are expected to be assertive, to stand up for themselves, to be ambitious and settle for nothing less than what they want because, well, *men will be men.* Women, on the other hand, are expected to be the nurturers, to look after those rambunctious boys/ambitious men and others.

Advocating for other people, friends, family, co-workers, is acceptable behavior for a woman, hence our success at negotiating salaries for others. To advocate for ourselves, however, well, isn't that a bit *selfish*? *Not* what a woman should be doing?

Even if we pride ourselves on being feminist, not falling foul of the patriarchy and its limitations, there's no denying that we are unconsciously taught to believe that certain behavior (advocating for others) will be met with approval, while the opposite (standing up for ourselves) is often met with rejection.

It's a hard habit to break, and many studies show that we haven't mastered it yet.

We'll be examining this whole issue in much more detail in chapter four and asking how we can succeed and avoid the gender bias at the same time. Is it even possible? We'll find out.

For now, however, let me just say that assertiveness *can* pay off in the end if we're brave enough to try and of course do it the right way. Take this study by the European Journal of Work and Organizational Psychology which finds that assertive dominant women in the workplace are paid more or better compensated than their less assertive female coworkers. Ditto, assertive men earn more than their less assertive male colleagues too. Proof, if it were needed, that assertiveness can take you places.

Of course, there is a caveat and it's the result of gender bias again. The study found that while assertive dominant women were considered more effective employees and paid more than their quieter female colleagues, they were **still paid less** than similarly quiet and unassertive men.

Boo, hiss. Blood boiling.

Perhaps not surprisingly, the 'nice' agreeable less assertive women were paid **less than everyone**. BUT here's the twist: they *believed* they were compensated more than they should be! What are these women thinking??? Well... The researchers theorized that less assertive women prioritize a harmonious workplace over demands for equal pay or fair compensation.

But haven't you got to wonder at a world where some women believe they don't deserve anywhere near as much equality as they should?

That pesky confidence gap really has a lot to answer for.

If you're one of those women who prefer to keep quiet for the sake of peace and harmony, let me demonstrate why you should find it within yourself to be assertive in our next chapter all about getting inspired to make a change.
We'll consider the benefits of being assertive such as less conflict and stress, plus what you could be missing out on by not being assertive. Clue: we're not just talking about money, but strong, supportive relationships too.

A strong, confident woman deserves all of that and more. So, read on to be convinced of your *real* worth...

Chapter 2 – Get Inspired to Make Chan_

"It is a mistake to look at someone who is self-assertive and say, 'It's easy for her, she has good self-esteem.' One of the ways you build self-esteem is by being self-assertive when it is not easy to do so. There are always times when self-assertiveness requires courage, no matter how high your self-esteem."
Nathaniel Branden

Why Make A Change?
In my last chapter, I promised that I would do my best to convince you of your real worth. Persuade you that you merit more, that you deserve to be heard, respected, cared for and appreciated.

In this chapter, I am going to prove to you how being a strong, confident woman will change your world – all our worlds – for the better.

You see, being assertive feels great. Asking for what you deserve, expressing your thoughts and feelings without anger, recrimination, high blood pressure (or the sick feeling at the pit of your stomach) changes your perspective on, well, pretty much everything.

It offers significant benefits to your health, wealth, happiness and sanity too. It can help with the control of your stress levels and boost your coping skills. Perhaps even more importantly, as our opening quote suggests, it has a hugely beneficial effect on your self-esteem and self-image.

How Does Assertiveness Help You To Become More Self-Confident?

There's little else better for your self-esteem than speaking up for yourself, taking control and influencing your world. If depression is sometimes caused by a lack of control, being assertive helps you to get it back and retain that control. Also, once things start to go your way because of your assertiveness, it will simultaneously increase confidence in yourself too. You will start a positive cycle of when one increases, so too will the other.

By being assertive, you have respect for yourself. You will have faith in your own opinions and the right to have and to express them. As a result, you will become more comfortable doing all of the above. You won't have to waste time going over what you wish you'd said in your head for hours on end!

Likewise, becoming more assertive gives you clarity; you begin to learn and confidently know who you really are. Your awareness of your own identity grows, your likes, dislikes, beliefs and values become solid. You develop a realistic self-image. You know that other people are not superior to you (as passive people often feel), but neither are you superior to them (a common belief among aggressive types). It's easier to appreciate and accept that everyone has their own personal preferences when you strongly believe we are all equal.

Because of your confidence in all of the above, you will not feel threatened if other people disagree or have a different opinion. You're will no longer coming from a place of fear (passivity) or competition (aggression), so you will also assess others view's more realistically. They are no longer a threat. Self-awareness, awareness of others and your empathy all grow stronger.

Another bonus – being assertive earns people's respect. How can it not? The very fundamental basis of assertiveness is that it is based on mutual respect. You respect YOURSELF – because you're choosing to stand up for your interests, expressing your thoughts and feelings. In return, you RESPECT OTHERS – being assertive rather than aggressive, demonstrates that you're aware of other people's rights and opinions and are willing to listen and to work on conflict resolution.

Being assertive will help you to cut out a lot of the stress you probably have in your life right now…

How To Have Less Stress and Have Stronger Relationships

I'm going to go out on a limb here and say that we could all benefit from less stress in our lives. Am I right?

Unless you're reading this book while sipping Mai Tais on a Caribbean beach or downing the Amber Nectar while swinging in a hammock on an Australian one, you'd probably appreciate less stress and conflict around you. To start down this path of less stress and better relationships, let's look into understanding the different types of behaviors you may currently be using.

Passivity = Conflict
You see passivity breeds conflict. You don't ask for what you want so, surprise, surprise, you don't get it. You're left

frustrated and fed-up, stressed and anxious about the lack of control in your life. You bottle it up, avoid communicating your thoughts and feelings, hence, quietly becoming angrier and angrier until one day you explode – and it comes out super aggressively.

Often the other party doesn't even know there's a problem until they are hit with it out of the blue. Cue weaker relationships and harder feelings… and the passive person feeling like a victim, closing in on themselves and dooming themselves to the same old scenario again and again.

Aggressiveness = Conflict
Aggressiveness too breeds conflict. The constant competition and need to win over everybody is exhausting. It alienates others; people who feel attacked will go out of their way to avoid you.
You may have a string of failed relationships behind you and have little social support. You might even see yourself as a victim, unable to realize it's your own behavior causing the problem.

I've worked in several high-pressure fast-paced mostly male environments and I've seen supreme confidence up close. It's always something I'm in awe of. I don't have a problem with men or women being sure of themselves but when it crosses over into arrogance and aggressiveness, that's where I draw the line.

One trainee of mine, let's call him Mike to spare his blushes, had trouble gelling with the team precisely because of his aggressive communication. His work was lackluster, but he was too arrogant to listen to constructive criticism. (Receiving criticism is often a trouble spot for people with aggressive tendencies). He wouldn't listen when told; he argued back, often insisting he was right to do what he did, despite better writers and much more experienced journalists trying to guide him. As a result, he didn't learn a thing because he refused to accept feedback.

His attitude didn't endear him to being part of the team either. He always had to win an argument – even against me, his boss. And he had a bad habit of invading personal space (particularly a woman's) as he all but puffed out his chest and stamped his feet, which often felt intimidating.

Now, I'd say I was a firm but fair boss (hopefully my team would agree) and I cared for my team but I have to admit something here: I disliked Mike intensely. I'm not proud of it – and it always makes me feel as bad. As if I was saying I didn't like a particular child (which I never would, of course!) – but I really struggled to warm up to him. Mostly because of the way he made me react to his aggressiveness.

The constant arguing was infuriating and exhausting; I couldn't ask him to do a single thing without there being some issue with it. Simply put, he didn't like answering to someone – anyone – else. Odd attitude for a trainee, you might think. I was also fed up of the repeated fire-fighting I had to do whenever he ruffled someone else's feathers.

I was a demanding boss, I admit to that but I never raised my voice to the team. They were professionals; even surrounded by a macho newsroom atmosphere with swearing and shouting the norm, I never succumbed. Until him. Mike pushed my buttons so much so, I lost my temper one day with him in front of everyone… and I never forgave him for working me up to such a point.

Yes, you might say that I should have controlled my emotions better and that I shouldn't have sunk so low, but dealing with an aggressive character – especially one so blind to his own flaws – pushed me over the edge. When we finally let him go (or rather pushed him onto another unsuspecting department as he had been pushed onto us) he was hurt. He had no idea of the trouble and ill feeling he'd caused. He believed he was the victim.

I've often thought about Mike over the years and wondered if he ever toned down his aggression. If he ever finally asked himself why other people didn't like him and did the hard work to examine his own actions and behavior. I hope he did, though I fear he didn't.

Don't be like Mike. Don't make other people dislike you; don't make them feel bad for reacting poorly around your aggression. Don't doom yourself to always walk alone.

Assertiveness = Balance
Try to be assertive, to gain balance. Assertive people are asking for what they want – with a much greater chance of achieving it – but they're not doing it at the expense of others. Less stress and conflict!

All sorts of things will seem to get easier when you learn how to be assertive… including being able to say that magic word, NO!

"The difference between successful people and really successful people is that really successful people say no to almost everything."
Warren Buffett

As the Mayo Clinic says, *"Being assertive… can help with stress management, especially if you tend to take on too many responsibilities because you have a hard time saying no."* You will be more able to manage friends, coworkers, your boss and your significant other, making everyday life that bit easier. Your lifestyle as a whole will become more balanced. Social anxiety, in particular, will reduce as you learn to face your fears, and your mood will improve. You will feel less angry towards others, feel comfortable saying 'no' and feel in control of your own life.

Sounds good, yeah?

And here's an extra bonus – you'll become more likable too. Research shows that assertiveness improves relationships, helping to make them more harmonious and satisfying. Remember those win-win situations; they don't just have to happen in the office or in other work settings, they can happen at home too. Expressing your needs directly also allows people to know where they stand with you.

I can't tell you how good it feels when you finally realize that people are listening to you and they respect your views. It's such a powerful feeling. I want that for you.

Other Benefits of Being Assertive

- **You will become more attractive to others** – I'm not saying that men or women will fall at your feet once you learn how to be more assertive, but assertiveness is certainly an attractive quality. Likewise, if other people perceive you as confident, they tend to assume you are also more capable and intelligent.

- **It allows you to become more open** – Passive people typically keep everything to themselves; you'll probably find that you feel like you don't know them very well. Likewise, if you're passive or lack assertiveness, other people might say the same about you. Being assertive allows you to get in touch with your feelings, helping you to understand yourself more. Suppressing emotions and desires is never healthy.

- **Accomplish more and get what you want** – You'll be shocked at how much more effective you are when you are honest about your opinions and needs. Being assertive means you act to make things happen, and you're much more likely to get what you want that way. It can be anything from speaking up when people are deciding which restaurant to eat at (if you don't suggest anything, it's unlikely that you'll eat where you want to) to asking for that pay rise or putting yourself forward for promotion.

- **Improved decision-making skills and win-win situations become the norm** – Here's something you may not have thought about before. If you're traditionally a passive person, chances are you have been unconsciously basing decisions in your life on the least confrontational solution or option. If you're an aggressive person, the opposite is likely true. Either way, your decisions are biased. By learning to find balance and be assertive, you'll develop a much more neutral stance and emotions won't rule your decisions from here on out. As a result, you will be more likely to seek win-win solutions for yourself and your counterparts.

  Remember:
  PASSIVE = other people win (and you resent them)
  AGGRESSIVE = you win (and other people resent you)
  ASSERTIVE = YOU BOTH WIN. Win-win solutions are us! Everyone's happy!

- **Being assertive gives you the strength to overcome negative thoughts** – Our thoughts and beliefs have a profound impact on our lives, whether we're aware of them or not. Someone who has negative beliefs, for instance, tends to see the negative in all situations and makes decisions based on negativity. Not surprisingly, this often leads to negative outcomes. Someone with positive beliefs, however, may well do – and achieve –the opposite.

Being assertive helps you to recognize, understand and overcome negative thoughts by showing that you can accomplish what you want to. Part of learning to become assertive encourages you to recognize your own internal dialogue and change it for the better.

- **It allows you to communicate confidently** – As we'll see in our next chapter on communication styles, being assertive is particularly useful when dealing with delicate or uncomfortable situations. It also earns the respect of your peers, and more confident communication puts you better placed for happiness in life and career success.

- **You can listen better** – Another important aspect of communication is listening. Genuinely listening to other people and being able to correctly interpret messages from others helps to reduce the chances of misunderstanding. It's hard to listen effectively if you're being aggressive – you're usually too busy trying to get your own point across.

  Passive people, too, are usually so fixated on not rocking the boat or even partially 'hiding' from people, they don't tend to be great listeners either.

  Assertive behavior – and active listening, a really useful skill I'll come on to talk about towards the end of this book – will help you to create scenarios where each party is happy and satisfied.

Assertiveness in the Workplace

Here's a perhaps surprising bonus of hiring more women managers in the highest ranks – they make a company more innovative!

Management and consultant Rocio Lorenzo discovered that innovation increases once the share of female managers in a company rises above 20%.

Jack Ma, of the Alibaba Group, China's biggest online commerce company, knows this only too well. His motto is: *"Hire as many women as possible. This is what we did, and this is the secret source."* His company is made up of 47% women, with 27% of them holding senior roles in the company. More than a third of its founders were women.

He's definitely doing something right. Alibaba went public with the world's biggest Initial Public Offering on the stock market in 2014. Since then, it has recorded profits of $15billion, has more global sales than Walmart and more active users/shoppers than Amazon (552 million compared to Amazon's 300 million). It has grabbed 60% of the Chinese e-commerce market so far and is still growing.

Known for its innovation, Alibaba is listed by Fast Company as one of their 'most innovative companies' and earned a praise-laden article in the Harvard Business Review under the title 'Alibaba and the Future of Business.'

Writing in Forbes, Daniel Newman says: *"From an AI chatbot to smart investments led by AI-enabled learning, Alibaba's innovations are currently unmatched."*

Being confident and assertive at work also has other benefits for you personally. Assertive people:

- Excel at selling and pitching their ideas to others.
- Gain the respect of the management team, and their own team because they are open to discussion and willing to share.
- Are comfortable with supervisors and the boss at work.
- Make great managers. They engender loyalty by treating people with respect and fairness, becoming someone people want to work with. As such, they manage co-workers and subordinates effectively, with empathy.
- Are more productive.
- Are pro-active problem solvers. Assertive, confident people are empowered to do whatever it takes to achieve the best solutions whilst respecting other people's rights.
- Can recognize and manage aggressive and/or passive behavior in others.
- Are less stressed, less anxious. You won't feel victimized or threatened if things go wrong, or don't go as expected.
- Enjoy a more balanced lifestyle, in control, as a result.

If you're missing out on any of this in your life and working environment now, isn't it time you made a commitment to change that? To continue on your path towards confidence and assertiveness (the first step of which is reading the rest of this book, of course!).

Look at what happens if you don't...

Not Being Confident or Assertive Means... You don't lean in.

Being Passive Means... You don't take care of your needs.

As Oprah said: *"When you don't stand up for what you need, you slowly strangle your spirit."*

There is evidence that women are socialized to be more passive (and men more aggressive) even from a young age. In 2006, two different research experiments aired on ABC's 20/20. The test subjects were aged 9-11 and were either one or two boys, or one or two girls. The footage broadcast was typical of how virtually every child reacted, said the researchers at the time.

- **Experiment One:** The children were given a glass of lemonade. Instead of sugar, salt had been added, making it unpalatable. The boys' reaction? Dramatic gagging and responses such as *'It's terrible, why did you give me this?"* In contrast, the girls drank it, grimaced, but said: *"That's good, thank you."*

  When asked why they lied about the lemonade, the girls said they didn't want to hurt anyone's feelings. The boys had no such qualms.

- **Experiment Two:** The children were given a gift-wrapped box and asked to open it. The presents inside were either a pair of socks or a pencil. Virtually every girl without fail responded, *"Thank you, I could use a pencil."* Not wanting to hurt anyone's feelings again.

  The boys' responses were more honest, if less polite. They typically opened the box and said, *"What a stupid gift!"*

What conclusions can we draw from this? For years, girls have been socialized to be people-pleasers, boys to be aggressive. Such extremes and lack of balance are mentally unhealthy and stressful. If girls defer to other's needs ahead of their own, they will be constantly frustrated and stressed.

If this is you, you're setting yourself up for a life of frustration. Chances are in order to get what you want, you'll end up resorting to unhealthy and indirect ways like hinting, passive-aggression, manipulations and suffering, or simply doing without.

Being Aggressive Means... You may suffer hidden consequences of your actions, such as the... *20-SECOND PAYBACK RULE.*

An aggressive person thinks in terms of win-lose (hint: they intend to win, and for someone else to lose). They are likely competitive, goal-focused and seek to earn points at someone else's expense. The notion of a win-win mentality or option wouldn't even occur to them.

But, it's not all roses even if they do get what they want. They may, for instance, feel guilty after riding roughshod over someone else's rights; they may also suffer the 20-second payback.

Coined by Synectics of Boston, MA, the 20-second payback rule refers to the length of time it takes for someone who feels disrespected to strike back. They may not actually achieve their payback in that time, but you can bet your bottom dollar that they've decided to go for it. Payback could occur in any form, whether it's skipping work or somehow sabotaging his or her opponent. There's a reason that experts in communication warn that aggressive people may win the battle but lose the war.

I don't know about you but neither of those end results appeals to me... and they shouldn't to you either. You are worth much more than that, and it's time you started believing it.

I want to finish with this quote from author Edith Eva Eger. It sums up the choices you face pretty effectively...

"To be passive is to let others decide for you. To be aggressive is to decide for others. To be assertive is to decide for yourself. And to trust that there is enough, that you are enough."
Edith Eva Eger

It is my hope that by the end of this book, you will have the confidence to realize that you ARE enough. We all are. In fact, as women we are extraordinary!

So, let's continue on our quest to make sure we never forget that again. Next up, let's assess your default communication style – are you passive, aggressive, assertive or passive aggressive? Let's find out...

Chapter 3 – Assess Your Default Communication Style

What Does Assertiveness Look Like To You?

Let me ask you a question: what does assertiveness look like?

Pretty tough to answer, isn't it?

I've talked a lot about the difference between being passive, assertive and aggressive so far in this book, but have you been able to identify yourself yet?

Do you know how you typically behave or react in any given situation? Being able to assess your own default communication style – and the possible drawbacks that may come with it – is the first step to changing it.

There are four distinct communication styles, and while we often use different styles in different circumstances, we tend to fall back on one particular style. That's especially true when we feel uncomfortable or unprepared. That's why it's so important to be able to recognize your default style.

For instance, if you don't take the time to recognize that your instinctive response is more aggressive than it is assertive, you could easily fool yourself into thinking you don't need to work on it. That you're already doing everything right, even when you're doing it way wrong!

Alternatively, you may try to convince yourself that you're reacting in the best way possible when faced with uncomfortable situations but in reality, you are letting your passive nature dictate your actions. You are not stepping up or leaning in… and you don't even know it.

Self-analysis is crucial to help you move forward, to boost your confidence and assertiveness and to hopefully improve your life as a result. So, let's find out what your default communication style is.

Consider the following situations and answer honestly how you'd react....

Scenario 1:
Someone cuts in front of you as you queue to pay at the supermarket. Do you...

- A. Do and say nothing, though you're not happy. Let them stay in front of you.
- B. Get angry. They obviously did it on purpose, who do they think they are??! Let them know how annoyed you are, by saying, *"Hey jerk, no cuts!"*
- C. Tap him or her on the shoulder and say, *'Excuse me, but I was here first'*. He probably didn't see you in line, so you give him the benefit of the doubt.

Scenario 2:
A coworker who likes to chat wants to discuss a personal matter with you but you're really snowed under with work and don't have time to talk. How do you react?

- A. You let her talk for as long as she wants, she obviously needs it. You'll stay late to make up the work.
- B. You don't have the time for this! She obviously doesn't respect you or your schedule. You say sarcastically, *"I don't have all the time in the world, you know?!"*
- C. You listen for a minute or two, then say, *"I'm so sorry you're having a rough time, but I don't have*

time to talk anymore right now. I have to get this presentation finished before the end of the day. Can we talk more after work?"

Can you see a pattern in the answers yet?

- Answer **A** in both scenarios, and there's no doubt you're a passive communicator.
- Answer **B** and your default communication style is aggressive – and ouch, by the way!
- Answer **C** and you are assertive and wise enough to try to find a balance between the two.

Every day you are faced with numerous situations just like these – and many which are more important – and you need to decide how to react to them each time. When you react without thinking, you will revert back to your default communication style. That's why we need to make sure your default style is productive, rewarding and likely to get you what you want. In short, we need to make sure it's more assertive.

Let me give you some more examples of passive, aggressive and assertive communication in case you're still on the fence about where you fall on the spectrum of assertiveness. I'm also going to add a fourth communication style – passive-aggressive.

I'm going to talk about the sort of language each style uses, the non-verbal cues you can use to assess your own and other people's natural communication preference, and summarize what those mean for you – i.e., what they tell us about your behavioral characteristics.

Finally, I'm going to include a section where you analyze how that communication might make other people feel –

this is a great way to see how effective (or otherwise) your communication is.

The Assertive Style – the Holy Grail of Good Communication

More likely to say:

- 'I'm sorry, but I won't be able to help you this afternoon. I have a dentist appointment.'
- 'Please, could you wind that window up? I'm feeling cold.'
- 'Please, could you turn the sound down. I'm struggling to concentrate.'

Nonverbal indicators:

- Open posture, relaxed, no fidgeting.
- Makes good eye contact.
- Voice is medium pitch and volume.
- Gestures are even and expansive.
- Respectful of other people's space.

Most likely to… (Behavioral characteristics):

- Achieve your goals without hurting other people.
- Take responsibility for own choices.
- Respect other people's rights, but also protective of own.
- Be able to accept compliments.
- Ask directly for what you need but accept there's a chance of rejection.

Makes others feel…

- They can take you at your word.

- They know where they stand with you.
- Respected by you, and respect for you.
- Able to give constructive criticism or compliments, because you can accept both.

The end result:

- Assertive communication is the best of all worlds and is likely to get you what you need.

The Aggressive Style – Bulldozing your Way Through Life

More likely to say:

- 'Do it my way!'
- 'Come on, jerk, do it right' (or any other form of name-calling)
- 'Oh, isn't that just perfect?' (said sarcastically, or any other form of sarcasm)
- 'You are crazy'
- 'You did that all wrong' (any form of blame)

Nonverbal indicators:

- Use a loud voice.
- Make big sharp/threatening gestures.
- Invade your personal space, stand 'over you'.
- Scowl, glare or frown, or any other visual indication of how unhappy he/she is.
- Make 'bigger' postures than others.

Most likely to … (Behavioral Characteristics):

- Be frightening, threatening or hostile.

- Be loud.
- Demand.
- Be belligerent and abrasive.
- Bully others.
- Be intimidating.
- Want to win at all costs, no matter if at someone else's expense.
- In short, this person believes their needs are the most important. It's as if they have more rights than anyone else. They will act as if they have more to contribute than others.

Makes other people feel….

- Resentful.
- Hurt and/or afraid.
- Defensive, making them withdraw.
- Aggressive, making them fight back.
- Humiliated.
- Less respect for the aggressive person.

The end result:

- Just look at the reactions of the people on the receiving end of the aggressive style. They have very strong reactions to what you say. And that's often the problem with aggressive communication – it's ineffective, mostly because people are so busy reacting to the way the message is delivered, that they fail to listen to the message itself.

  Your point gets lost. Likewise, if you become known as an aggressive person, other people will go out of their way to avoid you and will fail to report mistakes or problems to you because they fear being humiliated or exploited as a result.

I had a boss exactly like this. It's no exaggeration to say that he was the most difficult person I've ever worked with. He was brilliant, no question, and very talented – hence his important role in the company – but his lack of people skills was legendary.

It took very little for him to 'flare-up' – it could be over something as simple as someone not doing exactly what he wanted them to do… despite the fact that he had never told them how to do it. He expected them to read his mind, and when they couldn't (particularly difficult when he changed his mind so regularly, anyway), he would lose it.

By losing it, I mean he shouted, threw things (often at people), swore at them, insulted them, used the c-word far too often, even demanded I sack people at least twice a week. I didn't, of course. Now, if you're wondering how on earth someone like was ever allowed to operate (HR be damned), let's just say I worked in a very macho environment where a blind eye was turned to far too much.

Here's the interesting point though – he very rarely reacted that way with me directly. I could pretend it was because I was always perfect, but that would be a lie. No, I think it was because I made it clear at the outset that I would not put up with that sort of behavior aimed at me. From day one, I called him out on it. Even when I wanted nothing more than to run away and hide (yes, there were those days), I made myself stand up to him. I made a point of reacting assertively (and not aggressively), and he came to respect that. Otherwise, he would have walked all over me in the same way that he tried to do with everyone else.

I will tell you something honestly, however: it was exhausting. Being around aggressive people is phenomenally tiring, no wonder people choose to walk away.

(If you feel alone a lot of the time, or lack significant relationships in your life, it's worth asking yourself if your aggression may be the cause. Other people may feel the need to protect themselves against you. You may feel abandoned, but it's likely that your behavior is pushing other people away).

Anyway, I swear my blood pressure rose just from being in the same room as this man. He was one of the reasons I left the job in the end; I didn't want every day to be a battle.

I often wonder if he ever did the work to assess his own default communication style; something tells me he didn't. In fact, I'd guess a week's pay on it, because it's now 10 years down the line and my old boss – a talented, creative, very intelligent human being – is still exactly where he was when I left the company. With his education, skills, and ability, he should have been a shoo-in for promotion long before now. The fact that he seems to have reached his upper limit – his own personal glass ceiling – tells me his people issues are still at play.

The Submissive Style – Head Down, Avoiding Conflict

Most likely to say…

- 'I don't mind, you choose.'
- 'Oh, it doesn't matter/it's not important.' (even when it plainly is)
- 'You can have it if you want it.'

Nonverbal indicators:

- Speak with a soft voice.
- Keep their head down, making themselves as small as possible so they won't be noticed.
- Refuse eye contact.
- Fidget.
- Demonstrate the outward signs of anxiety.

Most likely to ... (Behavioral Characteristics):

- Act Apologetically.
- Avoid conflict.
- Struggle to make decisions or take responsibility.
- Fail to stand up for their own rights or needs.
- Behave as if other people's needs are more important.
- Yield to others.
- Blame others, feel like a victim.
- Be too uncomfortable to accept compliments.

Makes other people feel....

- Exasperated and frustrated.
- You don't know what you want.
- They can discount you.
- Guilty.
- Able to take advantage of you.
- Resentful (attempts to help a submissive person are often rejected).

The irony about submissive people is that they spend all of their time trying to please people and avoid conflict but in the end, their low energy and victim mentality – most often coupled with a reluctance to try new initiatives that could improve things – simply ends up frustrating people.

The Passive-Aggressive Style – 'Cut Off Your Nose to Spite Your Face'

As this will be the first time, I mention the passive-aggressive communication style in any detail, let me first explain what it is. In essence, as the name implies, this is a mix of both the passive or submissive style of communication above, along with a (more subtle) indirectly aggressive style.

Here the passive-aggressive person appears passive on the surface, but they are actually angry underneath. They don't have the ability to be out-and-out aggressive like the people above, but they act out that aggression in more indirect ways. Think manipulation, sulking, being two-faced, sarcasm, a subtle undermining of the person at the center of their resentment. The irony is by acting this way, they may actually end up sabotaging themselves as well.

Most likely to say...

- 'You can do it; you always know better anyway' – said with a hint of sarcasm.
- 'Sure, take the car today. I'll just be late; my job is obviously not as important as yours anyway.'
- 'Fine, whatever.' (sulking)
- 'I'm not mad.' (denying their feelings)
- 'You look very good for your age.' (backhanded compliment)

Nonverbal indicators:

- Speak with a (false) sweet voice.
- Look sweet and innocent too.
- Pretend to be friendly, and get close, touching, etc....

- Stand hands on hips when being sarcastic.

Most likely to … (Behavioral Characteristics):

- Be sarcastic.
- Sulk.
- Gossip.
- Be devious.
- Complain/Whine.
- Be two-faced.
- Be untrustworthy.
- Manipulate.

Makes other people feel…

- Angry
- Hurt
- Confused

Who Dares Wins?

There's a quick way to summarize the four different communication styles, and that's by looking at who intends to 'win' in a typical situation. For instance, an aggressive person wants to win at all costs and usually at someone else's expense.

Summary:

- Assertive – I win, you win
- Aggressive – I win, you lose
- Submissive/passive – I lose, you win
- Passive aggressive – I win, you lose

Of course, that doesn't mean that these people always get what they want. Walking away from an aggressive person, for instance, instead of playing along, can interrupt their competition and ruin their plans.

Is your Communication Style Hurting Your Career?

While you're doing the self-analysis needed to identify your default communication style, here's another aspect to examine – how to tell if your communication approach is hampering your career.

Here are some tell-tale signs that your style needs some TLC.

- **People respond poorly to your words or don't respond at all** – Here's the good thing about communication – you can usually tell how well it's received by judging the immediate outcome. What happens when you run the staff meeting, or when you speak up in the boardroom, for instance? Do your colleagues respond well; do they support your ideas, follow-up on your suggestions? Or do they criticize them and shoot down your initiatives? Do you engender trust or disloyalty?

- **Colleagues don't listen** – There's something wrong with your communication if your suggestions are ignored, or not listened to and your point doesn't get made. If people listen well, and the conversation builds on what you've said, it's a strong sign that you are communicating effectively. On the other hand, if the conversation immediately veers away from your suggestions – or worse, doesn't even acknowledge them – then you need to work on your assertive communication skills.

- **People respond negatively to your words** – Here people actually respond negatively to your words; there's a backlash when you speak. Part of being a powerful communicator is knowing your audience: if you're experiencing backlash when you talk, you are either threatening someone inadvertently, or you haven't considered the repercussions of your ideas. True, some people may have hidden agendas but it's your role as an assertive, strong communicator to identify those and understand what impact your words will have on other people. Once you recognize that, you can work to tackle it.

- **You feel invisible** – Do you leave meetings frustrated that people talk over you, or forget that you even spoke? That's a sign that your 'power' as a contributor isn't strong enough, and you can work on that but first, you must understand the powerplays and the power dynamic at hand. Once you appreciate that, you can take steps to address your own lack of it.

- **No-one takes you seriously** – In order to develop your career, especially in leadership, you need other people to take you seriously. That doesn't just happen because you want it to. You need to demonstrate why people should take you seriously, which means communicating in a way that people believe you know what you're talking about. You need to learn how to demonstrate your professional abilities and skills through your communication and how to communicate with 'clout'.

So, what can you do if you recognize yourself in any of the above? Well, here's the good news – you can change it. Don't fall into the trap of thinking' oh well, it's just my personality, I can't change' because you CAN.

That's what I want to be the takeaway from this chapter: you can use whichever communication style you want. So, if you recognize that you tend to be an aggressive or passive communicator, you can change it. You're not stuck with it. Likewise, if you experience any of the above when speaking to your colleagues, you can work to change that too. Your default communication style doesn't have to define you if you don't let it.

Yes, it will take a high degree of self-awareness, but you've already started the process with this chapter. Once you recognize yourself in any of the above (and this process only works with absolute self-honesty), it's much easier to then identify any shortcomings or areas to improve in order to communicate more assertively.

It's a commitment worth taking if you want to reduce stress and conflict, limit anxiety in your life and strengthen your relationships. It will help you to diffuse anger and forge better relationships in your personal and professional lives.

You will find help, tips and practical suggestions crammed throughout the second part of this book.

While you work on the above, here's a good rule to live by:

The success of your communication is YOUR responsibility.

If someone doesn't respond the way you want them to, perhaps they turn away or react aggressively towards you, you need to look at your own communication first. Their reaction may well be caused by something you did, said or implied.

If you tend to blame others for your communication mishaps, for instance, remember the rule of effective communication above and look to yourself first.

Likewise, if you experience any of the above from your colleagues – lack of respect, failure to listen, negative reactions, poor responses – you need to be accountable. You need to own your part in it. In short, don't blame others for your failings.

That said, you also need to remember that people may have different communication styles to you, so if someone hardly responds to your garrulous approach, it doesn't necessarily mean that your communication has failed. They may just be an introvert and less prone to outward reactions. Likewise, if someone else is shy, try not to bark at them.

The key is to make sure your communications convey what you want it to and gets the reaction you desire. The truth of the matter is that we can't NOT communicate – as you've seen by the examples I gave above, communication isn't just about the words you use, but the way you say them, and everything else besides. The way you roll your eyes, the gestures you use, the facial expressions you wear, the way you position your body… they all communicate something. They key is to make sure they communicate what you want them to.

Our communication style and approach to others conveys a huge amount about how we view ourselves and others. It's intricately tied into how well we lead and manage people, as well as our sense of power and worth.

For many professional women, powerful and authoritative communication in the professional arena doesn't come naturally… and we're going to delve a little more into the why of that in our next chapter...

Chapter 4 – Confidence & Assertiveness: The Truth

Before we move onto the second part of this book, offering strategies to build confidence, I think it's time we look in more detail about why women sometimes hesitate to be assertive. Is it purely because we're not confident enough? Is it because we fear we're not good enough? Or is there something more insidious at play?

It's important to examine the reasons behind our lack of assertiveness as a gender because otherwise, how can we change things? There are likely circumstances at hand that you may not be consciously aware of. It's only by bringing them out into the open that we can tackle and overcome them.

In my opinion, a few things hold women back from being assertive – including our own bad habits, personality traits, past experiences, fear of failure, being unable to say no, and our communication styles. I'll talk about these towards the end of this chapter.

However, by far the biggest barrier to assertiveness is culture, which is what I want to talk about now. You see, women's' lack of assertiveness isn't actually about women per se… it's about how society stereotypes women.

<u>Cultural and Societal Barriers To Women's Assertiveness</u>
It may seem like a cop-out to blame society and outdated stereotypical thinking for women not being confident or assertive enough but the truth is that such stereotypes do exist and have an influence on all of us. Whether you're consciously aware of them or not, the chances are cultural

stereotyping has impacted you in your daily life many times as an adult (and no doubt as a child too).

Let's think back to the 'boys will be boys' and 'girls will be nice' mantra that we are encouraged to follow in childhood. Girls are expected to be nice, to listen to their parents, and to behave well. While boys… well, boys get away with everything. I have a younger brother, I know! It's ok for boys to be naughty, to be loud, high-spirited and boisterous. In contrast, if girls act the same, they are often made to feel shame.

Fast forward into adulthood and women already know that certain behaviors – looking after others, being nurturing, being quiet – is met with approval. While the opposite is met with disapproval or rejection. Such stereotypes feed directly into the *'Confidence Gap'* that we talked about in chapter one.

They also influence how we view leadership. It's no coincidence that typical leadership attributes are also stereotypically male. Attributes such as ambition, competition, and assertiveness. At the same time, stereotypical feminine traits such as nurturing, collaboration and homemaking are discounted as effective in traditional leadership. Note, I'm not personally arguing that they don't matter in leadership; after all, what is mentoring if not a little nurturing? Likewise, I once worked with a female head of Tech and Development and she was appreciated by her team in part because she 'stood up for them' when needed in the wider company. Possibly not something they would expect a man to do.

For the reasons above, however, if you ask people to imagine a leader, they tend to subconsciously imagine a man. Ditto if you ask them to picture a doctor, too. This unconscious preference for male leaders contributes towards the glass ceiling women struggle within their professional careers.

The Gender Bias Backlash is another reason for it.

What Is The Gender Bias Backlash?
Gender Bias Backlash... even the words make my hackles rise. Nothing infuriates me quite as much as the notion that when women do behave assertively, especially in the workplace, they receive backlash.

And when men behave the same, it's normal. Not even a raised eyebrow!

Why? Because gender stereotypes typically expect men to be dominant, assertive and competitive, and women to be submissive, nurturing and warm. Any woman who goes against stereotype (and to be fair, some men too) suffer the gender backlash... negative economic or social reprisals.

Grrr.

I want to tell you to ignore it, to power through it but the reality is that it can impact your career – even though it shouldn't – so it's not something we can dismiss lightly. As unfair as it is, you need to know the unwritten 'rules' of assertiveness so that you can decide when to break them. Or how to work around them.

Here is Gender Bias in the nutshell:

Admirable Male Traits:

- Powerful

- Confident
- Worthy...

These are the sort of words likely used to describe assertive men. When they ask for a pay rise, express opinions or ask questions, they are seen in the above light,

In contrast, whenever women ask for a promotion, raise concerns or express their opinions, they face backlash, whether spoken out loud or not. These women may be viewed as:

- Aggressive
- Dominant
- Bitch
- Not nice...

These are the sort of words and thoughts that are often used to describe assertive women because they are pushing against and not fitting a gender stereotype.

Infuriated, yet? You should be.

The Double Bind
This backlash leads to the Double Bind for women: A tenuous position AND likeability issues.

Take this scenario...
Leadership theory suggests that for women to become leaders they must display traits commonly associated with leadership, such as assertiveness. However, studies also demonstrate that when women do exhibit typically 'masculine traits' such as – you guessed it, assertiveness – they are less liked than men demonstrating the same traits.

Let's say that again:
A man and a woman walk into a boardroom (sounds like the start of a joke, doesn't it? Unfortunately, it's not!). The man is assertive, gets his point across... and that's OK. People still like him. Why wouldn't they?!

The woman behaves exactly the same – and... people don't like her anymore.

The woman is penalized for the exact same behavior as a man... simply, because, well to put it crudely, she can't pee standing up. She is not fitting into the neat, nice female gender box.

Don't believe me? A study in Psychological Science found men who expressed anger in a professional setting received a boost to their perceived status (giving them a higher status), with their anger attributed to external circumstances.

In contrast, women who did the same were judged harshly, were accorded a lower status (with lower wages to match) and were judged as less competent. Their anger was also attributed to internal characteristics rather than external circumstances, meaning they were branded 'an angry person' or 'out of control'. This lower status was conferred on women no matter what rank they were, i.e., both female CEOs and female trainees were judged the same.

Of course, I don't advocate getting angry at work but it is an effective demonstration of what women face if they speak up in their professional lives.

Here's another pretty famous example.

A Harvard Business Review study gave an identical case study about the career of a real-life entrepreneur to two groups of students. The case study documented how this person had achieved success as a venture capitalist by using their networking skills and personality. The only difference between the two case studies? One was called Howard, and the other Heidi. (The case study was based on real-life Heidi Roizen). Otherwise – let me reiterate – the text was exactly the same for both groups.

Researchers then measured how the two case studies were received, asking a set of questions to determine what people thought of Howard/Heidi's personality. Both were thought to be equally competent, BUT Howard was liked more, while Heidi was considered selfish and not 'the type of person you would want to hire or work for.' In short, she wasn't liked. For no reason other than she was a woman.

Ouch. Poor Heidi.

In her book, **Lean In,** *Sheryl Sandberg* referred to this study and concluded: *"This experiment supports what research has already clearly shown: success and likability are positively correlated for men and negatively correlated for women. When a man is successful, he is liked by both men and women. When a woman is successful, people of both genders like her less".*

The Likeability Issue In Politics
No one knows this better than Presidential candidate Hillary Clinton. During the elections, poll after poll demonstrated that people found her competent but NOT likable. There was even a book published by author Ed Klein, entitled: *'Unlikeable: The Problem with Hillary.'*

Adrienne Kimmell, of the Barbara Lee Family Foundation who campaigned to get a woman into the White House, told the Boston Globe that, *"female candidates who aren't likable also are viewed as less qualified for the post, even if the candidate has excellent credentials."*

Being unlikeable damaged Hillary's electability. No matter what your politics, you can't say the same was true for Trump, can you? Mr. Nice Guy, he was not. Every time he made a nasty remark, his poll figures climbed.

And that summarizes the sexism at the heart of the likeability issue. The Barbara Lee Family Foundation found that women had to be seen favorably to garner votes. In the 2010 gubernatorial contests, for instance, when women opposed each other, the more 'likable' woman won 9 out of 10 times. When men ran against each other, however, likeability wasn't a factor and didn't predict the outcome.

In her book, Lean In, Sandberg also wrote: *"I believe this bias is at the very core of why women are held back. It is also at the very core of why women hold themselves back. When a woman excels at her job, both men and women will comment that she is accomplishing a lot but is 'not as well liked by her peers'. She is probably also 'too aggressive,' 'not a team player', 'a bit political'; she 'can't be trusted' or is 'difficult'."*

Faced with this gender bias backlash, women have a choice: speak up and risk potential judgment or rejection or stay quiet and never move upwards or forwards.

Not a great choice, is it?

The Double-Bind In Performance Appraisals

Women are not only penalized for being assertive in the workplace but as I mentioned earlier, the language used to describe them – especially when they reach leadership level – is distinctly different to that used to describe men. As we all know, language is powerful because of the associations that it evokes, and in this case, the image it paints of the person behind the words.

Consider these positive words commonly used to depict men in performance reviews (according to an analysis of 81,000 performance evaluations by HBR.ORG)

- Analytical
- Competent
- Athletic
- Dependable
- Confident
- Versatile
- Articulate
- Level-headed
- Logical
- Practical

Now consider these positive words commonly used to depict women in the same performance reviews.

- Compassionate
- Enthusiastic
- Energetic
- Organized

And… that's it!

Surely, they could have found a few more words!

Note how, even when the women are critiqued positively, they are praised for the 'softer' skills. If you're a boss faced with having to lay off a worker, who would you let go? The one who is Analytical and or Competent, or the one who is Compassionate and or Enthusiastic? It's probably not going to be the former, is it?

Now let's take a look at the negative words used to describe men and women, according to the same analysis.

Negative words used to describe men in performance evaluations:

- Arrogant
- Irresponsible

Negative words used to describe women in performance evaluations:

- Inept
- Selfish
- Frivolous
- Passive
- Scattered
- Opportunistic
- Gossip
- Excitable
- Vain
- Panicky
- Temperamental
- Indecisive

Now they can think of plenty of words to describe women! Harsh, isn't it?

And do you imagine they would ever describe a professional man as frivolous, excitable or vain? No, neither do I. So why is it acceptable to describe a professional woman in that way?

It all comes back to gender bias.

These are all real performance evaluations, by the way. More than 80,000 of them. They're not just examples I plucked out of thin air for demonstration purposes.

Here's what else we know about the double-bind:

Women receive negative 'personality' criticism – often for coming on too strong, being 'bossy' or warned about their tone – in nearly 75% of performance reviews.

In a study highlighted on Fortune, examining 248 reviews from 180 people in tech across 28 different companies, Textio CEO Kieran Snyder discovered that 87.9% of the reviews received by women featured negative feedback. This compared to 58.9% of the reviews received by men.

That wasn't the only difference, however – she found that men's negative feedback was typically shared constructively, with suggestions for developing additional skills. Women's negative feedback, however, also focused on personality critiques, such as being too abrasive, critical, judgmental or even failing to step back to let others shine.

She discovered words such as bossy, strident, abrasive and aggressive used to describe women's leadership qualities, and irrational and emotional used when they objected. In her data set, abrasive was used 17 times to describe 13 women. In contrast, the word aggressive was used only three times in men's reviews, and two examples of those were encouraging the men to be more of it.

She writes: *"This kind of negative personality criticism – watch your tone! step back! stop being so judgmental! –*

shows up twice in the 83 critical reviews received by men. It shows up in 71 of the 94 critical reviews received by women." She summarized by saying, *"Men are given constructive suggestions. Women are given constructive suggestions – and told to pipe down."*

Another disheartening discovery was that it didn't matter if the reviews were done by male or female bosses – they critiqued women the same.

Despite all the advances in recent years, feminism and sexism laws, it sometimes appears as if we haven't advanced beyond the stereotypical 'emotional' woman having fainting and conniption spells whenever a situation becomes stressful.

Why else would it be considered ok to call a senior woman 'hysterical', as happened very publicly to California Senator Kamala Harris? Harris was interrupted and ridiculed by her male colleagues twice in one week on the national stage and called 'hysterical' for behavior that was assertive and forceful – but clearly not hysterical.

The unconscious and conscious gender bias at play here led to a woman being shut down by her male colleagues, who treated her as if she was a child who needed scolding. And yes, this was in the 21st century (2017 to be precise).

Forceful assertive women are further penalized as often their perceived worth will also fall. New York Times bestselling authors and behavioral science researchers Joseph Grenny and David Maxfield share their research on this issue in Forbes. Discussing their study, they state that workplace gender bias is real and that women who are judged 'forceful' or 'assertive' are penalized by a drop in their perceived competency of 35%, while their perceived worth falls by

$15,088. This compares to 22% and $6,547 in men respectively. They argue that, *"this significant difference reveals a true gender bias that prohibits women from succeeding fully in leadership and management roles where assertiveness is, of course, a crucial behavior."*

Reading these types of figures can destroy and suck all the motivation out of you, as it appears women are damned if we do and damned if we don't.

The Solution

So, what's our solution? Given all that seems to be against us when we do try to be assertive or speak our minds, how do we handle it? Do we curl up in a corner and accept the status quo? (I'm hoping you're shouting 'no' right now!). Or do we call out both those men and women (because the gender bias is, unfortunately, perpetuated by both genders) who penalize us for being assertive?

I think we have three options, and I'll go through them each one by one.

Solution 1: Don't Even Try
Why even bother learning to be assertive when you're only going to be judged negatively for it? Life's easier if you just set your sights a little lower and be the 'nice' employee instead …

Said no-one who ever succeeded at life, ever!

Confidence and assertiveness are important for more than just your professional career, and I truly believe it can make you a happier person in the long run. It's fine, of course, if you genuinely don't want to chase that promotion at work. However, make sure you're doing it (or not doing it) for the right reasons. Namely, for you, and not because society has conditioned you into thinking you don't deserve more. Or because you're scared.

At heart, I think a lot of women will admit to wanting to be liked – we all have a basic human need for companionship and friendship, after all. So, it may be tempting to avoid rocking the boat and maintain your relationships with others rather than risk being disliked or judged because you asked for more or stood your ground. But is that really sustainable or healthy?

I consider myself a strong, assertive woman but my work friendships are also important to me. Giving up some friendships in order to become 'the boss' did bother me at times. When I walked into the bar after work with another department head only to find my entire team already there – and not one of them had invited me along – it stung a bit. As did the knowledge that I wasn't 'one' of them. As they say, it can be lonely at the top.

But employees have needed to vent about the boss from time immemorial, so I tried not to take it to heart. I also wasn't about to let it stop me from becoming an effective leader – and just in case you're wondering, I did get invited to the bar several times after that.

Having strong work relationships can make the day go smoother but it's not really a good reason to put yourself at the bottom of the pile. You can bet that a man wouldn't do the same!

Solution 2: Think 'To Hell With It! I'm Not Here To Be Liked Anyway!'

Many people will tell you that you don't go to work to make friends. You go to earn money, do a good job and to advance your own career. You don't need to be liked.

That's all well and good, yet this advice most likely to come from a man who hasn't faced any of these issues. Be aware that if you decide to bullishly forge your own path despite the possible negativity; the unconscious gender bias you face when being assertive may actually harm your career.

With evidence demonstrating that people perceive you less favorably when you're assertive, it may mean that you miss out on pay raises, promotions, and job opportunities.

There's a school of thought, for instance, suggesting that likeability is a bigger deciding factor in getting a job than capability. I must admit that when I hire people, I look for capability first but if there are two candidates with similar qualities, I will usually choose the one who will 'fit in with the company ethos' best. You could say that's the one with the highest likeability factor. (Of course, I also like to think I don't penalize candidates for being assertive, either; in fact, I welcome it. Though I can't necessarily say the same if they step beyond assertiveness and into aggression.)

At the very least, you will need allies in leadership, so it may benefit you to tread cautiously.

Solution 3: Walk A Middle Path
I would dearly love to recommend to every woman that they should ignore the gender bias inherent in male-female relationships and in professional life. After all, why should we hold ourselves back just because it might make other people feel uncomfortable?

I would like nothing more than to tell you to 'go for it' – to wield your assertiveness like a weapon, pushing everyone who objects out of your path. Part of me is so angry at the very notion that such sexist stereotypes still exist today that I want to blast them out of your way.

But, in my calmer guise, I must recognize that these things do exist and that you have to steer around, through and over them – you have to be smarter and use more guile. Likewise, it's not just society's stereotypes at play (the macrosystem), but the microsystem as well, namely the supervisors, bosses, and colleagues surrounding women who also influence how women view themselves and the choices they make in the workplace. Not only do women internalize the macrosystem's expectations, but the microsystem does too – as supervisors, colleagues and bosses also evaluate women based on how they comply with gendered expectations.

The truth is that there's very little difference between the way a man and a woman lead or manage; the difference instead comes in how they are perceived. In order to avoid the assertiveness backlash for women, you may need to learn to work differently – to tread that fine line between masculine and feminine. Sometimes incorporating masculinity, sometimes femininity.

Not only do you need to be equally as competent as men, but you also need to demonstrate it in a way that isn't counterproductive to your own success.

In short, you need to be strategic and nuanced.

A meta-analysis of 63 studies, for instance, discovered that some of the backlashes against dominant or assertive women could be moderated by how it was communicated. Implicitly-conveyed assertiveness – such as non-verbal or para-verbal (speaking without hesitation, physically taking up more space, i.e., resting an arm on the chair, or standing more closely) – was not judged as harshly, or evaluated as negatively. This may be because it didn't consciously register as violating gender stereotypes.

Likewise, being assertive in the service of another person – or for the good of the company – was viewed as consistent with the woman's 'nurturing role' and therefore devoid of backlash. Framing your assertive behavior as an asset to the team, company or organization, therefore, is likely to be more effective and viewed more positively by all.

Finally, other studies show that women who choose to modify their assertiveness to comply with certain cultural expectations, such as politeness or by choosing relevant communication strategies to match the situation, also experienced better success.

Of course, those same women acknowledged the sheer amount of work needed to ensure negative feedback was minimized, pointing out that their male colleagues were not required to make a similar effort.

But rather than simply accepting and trying to work within this gender bias, shouldn't we seek to abolish it? Which brings me to one last thing we all need to do – to 'Flip It'.

Flipping It

International HR leader, Kristen Pressner of Roche Diagnostics in Switzerland, caused a stir when she confessed in her TEDx talk that she was biased… against other women. The woman whose job it is to protect employees admits she was shocked when she realized her own bias.

She told Kathy Caprino of Forbes, *"Particularly shocking to me was: I'd always thought that you could only have a bias against someone who was different than you. So it really struck me to discover to realize we can have a bias against exactly what we are. I am a woman leader and provider, yet simultaneously, I have a bias against women leaders and don't see them as providers."*

Having discovered this, she now recommends both men and women alike do the *'Flip It'* test on their assumptions. The test is simple in its elegance and effectiveness – before you judge someone (a woman, for instance) for her actions or behavior, flip it around: would you think the exact same thing if the recipient was male?

Often you wouldn't, which is how you know you're operating according to unconscious bias. And that's when you make a conscious effort to change it.

Here's a couple of examples where Flipping It showed obvious bias:

- When Hilary Clinton won the Democratic Party nominee for President, for instance, several newspapers put a picture of her husband on the cover. Flip it around – would they put a male candidate's spouse on the cover instead of the candidate? Heck no!

- This headline and story from BusinessWomanMedia.com: 'Internationally acclaimed barrister Amal Alamuddin marries an actor' is a great example of flipping. (The actor in question is, of course, George Clooney).

- Would anyone accuse a male senator of being 'hysterical' for communicating in the same way that Senator Kamala Harris did? No, no and no.

The Barriers to Destroy!

As well as cultural barriers to women's assertiveness, I've also touched on a few other obstacles so far that stop women from coming forward and speaking out – such as perceived roles, or failure to communicate effectively. The following issues are also potentially to blame for women choosing to be less assertive or passive.

- **The confidence killers** – Women have a few bad habits. Typically, for instance, we have a habit of assuming blame if something goes wrong while simultaneously crediting someone else or circumstances for our successes. (You may not be surprised to hear that men tend to do the opposite).

  For some reason, the search for perfectionism seems to be a female-only trait and there's no denying that it gets in our way. While men take risks we hang back, only attempting something if we believe we are supremely qualified. We fret over our performances – everything from our professional lives, cooking, relationships, friendships, even motherhood – and basically waste a lot of our time being less than assertive. And probably also, less than we could be.

- **Past experience** – People learn to behave a certain way by modeling their behavior on parents or other role models, or via experience. With the gender bias so intrinsic and yet so unconscious among many of our family, acquaintances, and peers, we may well have learned how to behave non-assertively as a result.

  Remember though, learned behavior can be difficult – but not impossible – to unlearn.

- **Personality traits** – I've mentioned this in passing before but it's certainly worthy of repetition. Some people believe they are either passive or aggressive by nature, that they were born with the relevant trait and there's little they can do about it. In most cases, that's simply not true. Everyone can learn to be more assertive, no matter what their so-called personality traits suggest.

I have made an argument for treading a wary path in this chapter considering the potential negative backlash you may face when trying to be assertive but the fact is that such gender expectations cannot continue. Work needs to be done – by everyone – to question and change them.

You may decide to make that your mission.

It is my role in this book to provide you with the tools you need to feel confident and to be assertive. Once you know how to do that, it's your choice how you choose to wield them.

That all starts with the next chapter and part two of this book: Strategies to Build Confidence…

Part 2 – Strategies To Build Confidence

Confidence = Assertiveness = Success

Let me open this chapter with a quote from Larae Quy, former undercover FBI counterintelligence agent for 24 years – and now coach, trainer and author on, 'Mental Toughness'. In her tips on developing self-confidence, she says: *"I learned quickly in the FBI that success would not make me confident. Instead, confidence would make me successful."*

There – that's the whole purpose of this book in a nutshell. Confidence can help your assertiveness, which in turn helps you to be successful. So, with that in mind, the second section of this book is dedicated to helping you to build confidence.

I'll show you how to develop a positive mindset; how to play to your strengths (did you know there's an actual place in the female brain where intuition lives?!); how to use body language, visualization and Emotional Freedom Techniques (EFT) to change your inner critic, and how to find confidence by taking risks and seeking courage.

We'll talk about all of that before moving onto part three of this book – which is crammed full of tips for being assertive at work and in your personal life, plus bonus advice on aspects of effective communication, such as active listening and effective speaking.

Before we can feel comfortable being assertive, however, we must first develop our self-confidence, which is why these middle chapters are so important.

This chapter, in particular, will focus on how to recognize and tackle the sort of negative thinking that prevents confidence – and I will show you how to develop the 'mental toughness' that Larae Quy advocates. It's pretty mind-blowing stuff, pardon the pun!

Chapter 5 – Start With The Mind: Developing A Positive Mindset

What is a positive mindset, and how can we achieve it? In essence, it comes down to stopping negative self-talk to reduce stress.

Self-talk is the constant stream of unspoken thoughts that run through our heads – *'Oh God, did I leave the oven on? That reminds me, I have nothing for dinner. I don't have time to make anything. What shall I do? Julie will be starving when she comes home from pre-school. She'll get grumpy. She won't let me do my chores. I guess I could put her in front of the TV for an hour or two. Or will that stunt her development? Am I harming my child? Am I a terrible mother?'*

That sort of thing!

You can see how quickly negative thoughts can spiral. Some of this self-talk may come from reason and logic (if you have left the oven on, you do genuinely need to get home quick!) but a lot of it can also come from misconceptions, worry or fear. You may have also inadvertently trained your brain to focus on the negative by dwelling on it so much.

Why does it matter? Because evidence shows that if your thoughts are mostly negative, your outlook on life is likely pessimistic. If the opposite is true and your thoughts are positive, you are likely to be an optimist. Optimists typically handle stress a lot better – and benefit from the positive benefits to health that brings.

Just look at these health benefits of positive thinking:

- Better coping skills during stressful times.
- Better psychological and physical wellbeing.
- Lower rates of depression.
- Better resistance to colds.
- Improved cardiovascular health.
- Longer life spans.

Wow, that really makes a difference, doesn't it! Researchers don't entirely know why thinking positively brings about these health benefits. However, they theorize that being mentally able to deal with stress better reduces the amount of physical stress on your body. Optimistic people may also tend to live healthier lifestyles.

Either way, thinking positively is the best way to a good mindset.

So, how can we achieve it?

Recognizing Negative Thinking

Thinking positive sounds simple but it's not always so easy to do. Fears, worries, concerns, jealousy, anxiety, stress… they all conspire to take us away from the positive and instead dwell on the negative. It takes considerable awareness and conscious thought to push that negativity away and revert back to a state of grace.

The first step towards doing so is to recognize when negative thinking is taking over. Let me ask you a few questions?

When something happens, do you filter out the positive and magnify the negative? If you've had a great day at work, for instance, do you sit at home, not thinking of everything you achieved, but dwelling on the few things that you didn't manage to get done?

Do you automatically picture or anticipate the worst possible outcome? If your child falls, for instance, do you automatically assume they've banged their head and need a trip to the ER, or do you just assume it will be a scrape?

If one small thing goes wrong in your day, do you assume the rest of the day will follow badly?

Do you tend to personalize things, and blame yourself when things go wrong?

Do you feel like a failure unless things go perfectly for you? Is there a middle ground, or is everything simply good or bad, polarized?

If these are things that you struggle with, you're letting negative thoughts crowd out the positive ones. You need to learn how to turn that negative thinking into positive thinking.

Turn that Frown Upside Down – Create a Positive Mindset

Before I recommend ways to encourage positive thinking, let me just say one thing: you are changing habits here, and in doing that it's not going to happen overnight. They say it takes an average of 66 days for you to learn a new habit. Time is irrelevant, really, but what it does mean is that it will require fortitude, constant self-awareness and determination to make the change. Don't be disheartened if you slip backward at times. The key to a positive mindset is to track your thoughts and adjust them whenever necessary.

If you have ever tried mindfulness, it teaches us that the 'return' is important. When you notice your mind has strayed to negative thoughts, bring your attention back to the present and to something more positive.

How to focus on positive thinking:

- **Talk positively to yourself** – Be kind to yourself and live by one rule. Never say anything to yourself that you wouldn't want to say to a friend, neighbor, colleague, family member, or even a stranger… to anyone else really. If a negative thought encroaches, evaluate it rationally and respond with positive affirmations about yourself.

- **Check your thoughts** – At several times during the day, stop whatever you're doing and question what you're thinking. If you're thinking negatively, make it your mission to put a positive spin on things.

    Examples could include:

    Negative – *I've never done this before, what if I can't do it?*
    Positive – *I can learn something new.*

    Negative – *I can't do this.*
    Positive – *Let's try it again.*

    Negative – *No-one talks to me.*
    Positive – *Let's try to open up the lines of communication.*

- **Memorize positive words** – This might sound crazy but it works. By memorizing lists of positive words, you force your brain to recognize them more easily thus making them more accessible and easily activated. By doing this, you can make other positive thinking strategies easier to apply.

- **Exercise for 30 minutes on most days of the week** – Exercise helps to 'workout' residual stress chemicals floating around in your body, while simultaneously releasing positive mood-boosting chemicals.

- **Seek out positive people** – Surrounding yourself with positive people who you can trust to give you helpful feedback is a good step towards developing a positive mindset. In contrast, negative people can not only increase your stress levels but make you question how you can cope.

- **Don't minimize your successes** – Remember what I said in our last chapter – we women tend to blame ourselves when things go wrong but give others the credit when they go right. Stop that! Right now!

  Give yourself credit for your successes, no matter how small. Take note of your wins and celebrate a little. Don't give in to the temptation to say things like 'well, anyone could do it' or 'I got lucky.' You didn't get lucky; you worked hard. And even if other people could do it, they didn't. You did.

- **Label your thoughts** – Here's a way mindfulness can help you tackle negative thinking – by simply recognizing that thoughts are just that – thoughts. Nothing more, nothing less. You do not have to believe them, nor engage with them, nor indulge them in any way.

  You are not your thoughts.

  By doing this, you take away their power. You put a certain

distance between yourself and your thoughts. So, while you can then acknowledge that you are having a thought, you don't need to give it the loaded meaning you usually do. You can label them neutrally. This is particularly useful when you want to reframe your thoughts like below.

- **Reframe your negative thoughts** – I'm a big fan of NLP – Neuro Linguistic Processing – precisely because of its position on things like this. NLP proponents believe you can retrain your brain by recognizing negative thoughts and making a concerted effort to change them.

Real Life Case Study – Maria

Maria, 34, struggled with negative thoughts after losing her job.

"I would consider myself quite a positive person before then," she says, *"but losing my job really knocked my confidence. I put my all into that job! I mistakenly believed I was important to the company. But when it came to letting people go, I was one of the first.*

"I found that really hard to deal with. My job was also my identity and the job market was horrendous then, so it seemed impossible to get a new job. But who was I without it?

"I started to have negative thoughts. Not anything terrible, not anything life-threatening or anything like that but I started to feel worthless. I would think 'I must have been rubbish at my job' or ask myself 'why didn't they like me?' I'd then feel guilty at being so negative – because it was so unlike me before – and I'd dwell on those negative

thoughts, effectively repeating them over and over again.

"Soon I'd convinced myself that it was my fault I was made redundant, but there was no point me trying to do anything about it or to improve myself because there must be a fundamental flaw with me."

It was a chance meeting with an old friend – an NLP practitioner, as it happens – that turned it all around for Maria.

"An old friend of mine came into town, looked me up and asked to meet. I almost didn't go, I didn't socialize much by then, but I'm so glad I did. I ended up having a drink or two too many and it all came blurting out."

Maria's friend asked to see her again the next day and introduced her to NLP. *"She told me she could help; stupidly I thought she was going to offer me a job or something. But she told me about reframing my thoughts and stopping negative ones in their tracks."*

The idea behind NLP is to always be conscious of your thoughts and to recognize negative ones. *"She told me to allow them in only as long as it took to recognize them, to notice how they made me feel, what I saw, heard and smelled, and then to cast them aside, to put the thought away from me, somewhere distant. She suggested a few different ways of doing this, but I ended up finding my own way.*

"Whenever I recognize a negative thought, I hold out my hand in a stop sign – sometimes only in my head, other times in real life too – and I won't let myself finish it. Before, I almost had to finish the thought or 'live through' the outcome before I could move on but it's important to

never let it get that far.

"So, I stop the thought dead, imagine myself plucking the thought out of my body and mind, cleansing myself, as if it's a pulsing ball of light, and then I throw it away. I throw it far away from me, and it dissipates into the air. I never let it come back again. It's amazing how much lighter the body feels after that."

Maria's approach is one way to banish negative feelings. You could also choose a positive thought to replace the negative one, and visualize it suffocating the latter out of existence.

Whatever works for you!

Developing Mental Toughness

Let me tell you more about Larae Quy, the former FBI agent I mentioned at the top of this chapter. Quy coaches other women on mental toughness – and she certainly knows what's she's talking about. As a counterintelligence agent with the FBI for 24 years, she exposed foreign spies, recruiting them to work for the United States' Government. She faced stressful situations and uncertainty, risk and deception every day… and needed mental toughness to survive.

She now helps other women achieve the resilience of spirit and mindset that she cultivated.
She advocates taking small steps to build confidence – as she points out, *"mountains are climbed one step at a time, not by giant leaps"* – and facing inward to build courage and develop a strong mindset.

Her personal tips?

- Don't run
- Don't panic
- Face the situation
- Believe you can do it
- Fix it as soon as possible
- Waiting will only make the situation worse
- Now is the best time
- I am the best person
  (Mantra courtesy of LaraeQuy.com)

She also argues that there are certain things confident women will NOT do. These include:

- **Take their day for granted** – Practicing gratitude is a great way to keep things in perspective. Yes, there may be a lot of things to feel sad, angry or hurt about but there's also an infinite number of things to feel joy about – you just need to decide to look for them.

  Savor the good moments, don't be so busy that you let them pass. Stop to smell the roses, or to appreciate life's small pleasures. Hold onto those positive thoughts and emotions for as long as you can. Gratitude comes back to you in spades. Express gratitude at work, and it boosts respect and camaraderie. Be grateful for your partner and children and they respond in kind. Being grateful for what you have helps to keep you positive.

- **Avoid eye contact** – Confident women don't avoid eye contact; they relish it. They know they have the confidence to control the situation and spread their influence. We're going to be talking a lot more about eye contact and other forms of body language or non-verbal communication in chapter seven, where we'll be examining body language for confidence.

- **Stay in their comfort zone** – We all have areas of life we're more comfortable in or people were more comfortable with. There's nothing wrong with some comfort now and again but if you never step outside this comfort zone, it doesn't stretch you or allow you to develop as a person.

  Staying static tends to harm your confidence over time. Confident women want to gain knowledge and explore the world around them. Taking risks is hugely important to your self-confidence. As hockey ace Wayne Gretzky said, *"You miss 100 percent of the shots you don't take."* In chapter eight, we explore the notion of taking risks, seeking courage and finding confidence.

- **Fade into the background** – Confident women don't act like wallflowers or speak in hushed weak voices; they speak to be heard. That doesn't mean they're bossy, strident or any of the other names people like to throw at assertive women but if you have something to say, make sure people can hear it. (The opposite is also true – if you have nothing of worth to say about a particular topic, don't blab.)

  If you don't yet possess the confidence to do the former, act 'as if'. Simply pretend you do. Acting 'as if' helps to train the brain to believe it's true, and before long, you'll realize you're not even acting anymore. I talk a lot more about this – alongside EFT and visualization – in chapter seven.

  Finally, confident women don't…

- **Hang around with negative people** – I've touched on this already in this chapter above, but it's worth repeating. Larae Quy agrees with me that on the point that confident people surround themselves with positive people, rather than negative ones. The people you choose to associate with or to befriend will help to create an environment you will either thrive or die in. You are a person of value and you deserve to be treated as such. Positive people will be happy for all you can achieve; they won't be competitive or judging.

I hope the tips I've shared in this chapter will start you off on the road to confidence and assertiveness. Choosing to live according to a positive mindset is one of the most generous things you can do for yourself.

Positive thinking is much healthier for body and soul than crippling negativity. Its influence on confidence too is self-explanatory. Fill your head with negative thoughts – which usually attack you and your competence – and before you know it, you start to believe it. You feel less worthy.
In contrast, positive thinking can lift you up, persuade you of your worth and soothe your soul.

Up next... I teased you earlier by revealing that women's intuition is a hidden advantage in a special part of a woman's brain... that area of the brain is called the insula, and we're going to examine how it can help you to tune into your innate qualities as a woman.

Chapter 6 – Play To Your Strengths

Emotional Intelligence

So, this chapter is entitled 'Play to your Strengths' but perhaps I should recommend that you 'Play to your Strengths as a Woman'. You see, women are often criticized for being 'soft' or 'emotional' (remember our supposedly 'hysterical' senator earlier?) Other people may try to make it seem as if our natural instincts and talents are not important. People often seek to make women feel less than because we tend to be better than men at the interpersonal stuff.

We care, we mentor, we read people, we're intuitive, we often excel at Emotional Intelligence… these are not failings. These are strengths. They may not fit the stereotypical impression of a leader or a boss – someone who doesn't let emotion influence them, who is straight down the line, yes or no, black and white – but the truth is that these softer skills are much more valuable than you probably realize.

Emotional intelligence or EQ – the ability to recognize, understand and manage your own and other people's emotions – is now considered to be even more influential than IQ when it comes to success. According to one survey of hiring managers, three-quarters or respondents suggested they value EQ over IQ, the traditional measure of intelligence.

Employees with higher EQ scores have been shown to be also rated higher for leadership ability, stress management, job performance, job satisfaction, and interpersonal ability. All key measurements of how well you may do in your job or career – indeed, strong EQ skills are extremely valuable in all relationships, both at home and at work.

In his book Emotional Intelligence: *Why it can Matter More than IQ*, Daniel Goleman argued that EQ is just as important, if not more so than IQ at predicting success in life.

This is not a book about Emotional Intelligence, though I do recommend you read one if you want to find out more as it's a fascinating topic AND the great thing about EQ is that it can be learned and improved upon, unlike IQ which is fixed.

Women do typically tend to be stronger in this field than men, however, and I hope I've already demonstrated why you shouldn't shy away from it. You should play to it.

The Gender Divide in Emotional Intelligence
Before I go on to talk more about the gender divide when it comes to EQ, let me issue a caveat. This, by its very nature, is a broad-brush approach. We can't possibly talk about all men and all women here; we can only go on what the studies show us, and they tend to talk about averages or majorities.

There will be men that excel in Emotional Intelligence and intuition. Just as there will be women who potentially struggle with it. (Again, if this is you, you can improve your EQ. I'll talk briefly about that here and suggest initial ideas for improvement but entire books have been written on this topic alone, so I suggest you consider this an introduction and then seek further help).

So, are women more tuned into Emotional Intelligence than men? Studies suggest yes, they are, in many ways.

Emotional Intelligence essentially consists of four elements:

- Self-awareness (recognizing our own emotions)
- Self-management (managing our own emotions)
- Empathy (recognizing and reacting to other people's emotions)
- Social skills.

Most EQ tests suggest women on average are better at pretty much all of these than men (sorry guys), meaning we naturally have the skills for an emotionally healthy and successful life. There is one area where men may hold the edge over us, however: dealing with distressing emotions.

Tests show women excel at emotional empathy, feeling what someone else feels, for instance, which tends to foster chemistry and rapport. People strong in this skill make good counselors, teachers, and leaders of groups. This ability is located in a part of the brain called the insula – also the 'home' of intuition – more on that shortly.

Science shows us that when we empathize with someone, our brain mimics what that person is feeling, the insula then reads that pattern and tells us what the feeling is. The insula in women is thought to be highly tuned, hence our strong empathetic skills.

However, here's the difference between the sexes. If the feelings are strong, upsetting or disturbing, a woman's brain tends to stay with those feelings. In contrast, a man's brain senses the feelings for a moment before tuning out and switching to a different part of the brain that tries to solve problems. Meaning they want to solve the problem causing the upset in the first place.

Have you recognized it yet? This is a scientific explanation for why we women complain that men don't want to listen to our problems but are always trying to solve them instead! It turns out they can't help it; it's hard-wired!

Both positions can have value. The male approach is useful in situations where you need to stay calm and insulate yourself against distress in order to find an urgent solution. Alternatively, the female instinct to remain tuned in helps to support and nurture people in emotionally upsetting situations.

Research shows that people high in Emotional Intelligence make better leaders – probably why the leaders in the top 10% of business performance have similar EQ abilities, male or female, according to psychologist Ruth Malloy of the HayGroup in Boston. Those who have naturally strong EQ skills, or those who take the time to work on their EQ skills, make it to the top.

How To Quickly and Easily Improve Your Emotional Intelligence

Unlike IQ, the traditional measure of intelligence, which cannot be altered (you can learn more but your basic ability to learn remains the same), EQ or Emotional Intelligence can be improved upon. As I said earlier, entire books have been dedicated to doing just this, so this chapter can only ever touch upon the topic and you should seek further resources to continue your work in this field.

If you want to improve or even just be more aware of your EQ skills, there are some basic steps that you can take.

Remember, better EQ skills help with stress management, self-confidence, improved social relationships, and mental and physical wellbeing.

As a start you can:

Practice Being More Self-Aware
The first step to Emotional Intelligence is to be aware of your own emotions. You can do this by paying attention to how you feel at any given time of the day, and once you recognize your emotions, consider why you feel that way and how they are influencing you. Do they influence how you react to other people, for instance, or impact the decisions you make? Write them down if it helps.

Take the time too, to take stock of your emotional strengths and weaknesses. Do you communicate well with others? How often do you experience negative emotions, such as anger or impatience? Consider how you can deal with those shortcomings. It may help to realize that emotions are fleeting – before you react with anger or make rash decisions that could hinder your long-term success, consider that most things are temporary.

Aim for Self-Regulation
Once you have identified what you are feeling, and why and when, then the next stage is learning to deal with your emotions and how to regulate yourself. This will help you to adapt well to situations and express your emotions appropriately. You will also recognize how your reactions influence others.

To practice self-regulation, pay close attention to your words and actions and how you tend to respond to certain situations. If you tend to react quickly, teach yourself to slow down and make a calculated response instead for a rash one. Also, look for ways to manage workplace stress – both in the office and once out of the office.

Develop Strong Social Skills

Social skills are highly prized in all aspects of life, and people with impressive EQ skills also tend to have strong social skills because they can recognize other people's emotions and respond appropriately. To improve your social skills, you should develop a few special skills of your own, such as active listening *(see chapter 11)* and paying attention to non-verbal communication *(see chapter 7!)*. Honing your persuasion and influence skills will also help your career.

Don't Shy Away from Empathy

We've already seen how valuable empathy can be, particularly in understanding different dynamics between friends and colleagues. To work on your empathy, try to look at situations from another person's perspective, especially during disagreements. It may help you to find a middle ground. Likewise, be aware of how you respond to others, and whether you let them have a say, acknowledge their input and allow them to share their ideas. The work you've already done into identifying your default communication style will help here.

Be Motivated

One final aspect of Emotional Intelligence that I haven't mentioned before is motivation. People with strong EQ's tend to be motivated to achieve – and, crucially, to achieve goals for internal reasons as opposed to external rewards.

This involves being passionate about what you do, loving your work, appreciating new challenges, and being enthusiastic; you're not working towards your goals purely for monetary reasons or status. It goes deeper than that –

which, as you'll find out – is a stronger indicator of happiness. In order to achieve this sort of motivation, focus on what you love about your job and be inspired by it (don't dwell on the negative) and try to maintain a positive attitude. Positive optimistic people inspire and motivate others.

Women's Intuition: Is It Real?

"There is a voice that doesn't use words. Listen."
Anonymous Author

I mentioned earlier that intuition has a 'home' in the brain, in a section called the insula, which primarily deals with empathy, intuition, and self-image. But does 'women's intuition' really exist? Are women more intuitive than men? And if so, how do we take advantage of it, how do we play to that strength?

It turns out that the answer is *'sort of, and yes'* all in one.

It seems that women are much better, as a group, at reading non-verbal communication cues than men. In short, we're much more likely to pick up on subtle messages being sent by others, which you could argue is a form of intuition. We're also better at expressing our emotions through facial expressions, body movements and tone of voice too. It all adds to the notion that women have a special ability to intuit what others think and feel.

Let's look at the evidence:

Take this experiment to identify women's ability to read the body language signals of babies, as carried out by Barbara and Allan Pease, authors of *Why Men Don't Listen and Women Can't Read Maps.* Women were asked to watch 10-seconds of video of babies crying with no sound; they had to identify the emotion by visual cues only. Most of the women (who were mothers) identified a range of emotions from pain to gas, to exhaustion to hunger. How did the men (who were also fathers) do? Less than 10% could identify more than two emotions. Their results were described as 'pitiful'. It gets worse for men when grandparents were put to the test. Grandmothers scored between 50-70% of the mother's high scores, while the grandfathers struggled to even identify their own grandchild!

A University of Cambridge study into cognitive empathy – the ability to understand someone's emotional state at a glance – wielded similar results. 90,000 people were shown photographs of people's eyes and had to say what they believed their mood was. In the survey, women consistently outperformed men. A follow-up study in 2018 identified genes was also involved in cognitive empathy and again confirmed women were more empathetic than men. However, DNA did not explain the gender difference in empathy.

So, we can accept that as a group, women are more turned into non-verbal cues than men (not to say that all men are incapable of it, or that all women are strong at it). But why? How? If, as the University of Cambridge study proves, DNA doesn't explain the gender difference, what does?

The theory goes that it comes down to social power, or traditionally, women's lack of it. Women, the lower group in social power, have spent more time observing those above them in the pecking order and have become attuned to their nonverbal cues. In short, women needed to pay close attention to the dominant group, almost as a survival instinct. Just as Martin Luther King Jr once said that black people had to be sensitized to how white people felt in order to survive a racist society.

It has taken generations of practice and now women have developed a sensitivity to reading other people's emotional states, our own version of women's intuition. Growing up, girls too are encouraged to be sensitive, while boys aren't encouraged to listen to their feelings in the same way. So at least that gender bias we talked about earlier is finally paying off for us in some way!

As to how best to use it, trust your gut feeling. Whether at home, out and about or in the office, trust yourself and recognize that you have inner knowledge honed by generations of women prior to you. Your ability to pick up on subtle cues is historical and shouldn't be ignored. If you feel that something is wrong, listen to it.

If you don't feel comfortable when walking alone at night, for instance, pay attention to what your instinct is telling you and react to it. Don't talk yourself out of the warning or argue that you should be logical. Keep yourself safe.

Likewise, if you don't trust someone when making a deal, for instance, question and investigate. Be aware that men, however unfairly, may not react well to hunches based on feelings (mostly because they're incapable of the same leap), so you might want to suggest taking a closer look without revealing that you're basing it on intuition.

Recognize too that being able to decode nonverbal and subtle cues helps you to be a better friend, partner, colleague, mentor, and leader.

I'm personally a big believer in intuition and in following

your gut. After all, I left my country, my friends, and my family, determined to start a new life. This with a man I'd only ever spent four full weeks together out of the previous six months. There was nothing wrong with my old life, I'd been very happy but I just knew I had to do this. My inner gut feeling told me – very strongly – to take a chance and go for it. And I'm so glad I did. Ten years later, here I am, still in my adopted country, with the same man (now my husband and the father of my lovely children), extremely happy and feeling very blessed.

Listening to my intuition – that he was a good man, that we belonged together, I should take the chance (as crazy as it seemed) – was the very best decision I ever made.

I encourage you to listen to your gut too. It may genuinely change your life for the better.

Chapter 7 – Faking It 'til You Make It

How to Appear Confident

Building self-confidence doesn't always come naturally, you will usually have to work at it. Until it feels natural, however, you can 'fake it until you make it'. There are ways you can show confidence even if you don't feel confident... and even better, you can convince other people that you are confident. As a double whammy, you can also convince yourself at the same time to feel more confident as a result.

You have nothing to lose by trying it, and everything to gain!

Just by appearing self-confident you can encourage other people to see you in a positive light, helping you to earn more respect from peers, colleagues, bosses, co-workers, friends, and even your partner. People want to believe the impression you send out. You'd be surprised how much people judge from first impressions, whether you're walking into a restaurant to meet a date or heading into a business meeting.

In her book, The Essentials of Business Etiquette, Barbara Pachter writes: *"You are in control of [the message] you are sending out. I believe that if you project a confident, credible, composed image, people will respond to you as if you are all those things. Who cares what you are feeling on the inside?"*

Making minor adjustments to appear more confident helps you to wield more influence and win kudos. So, how can you show confidence even if you don't feel it?

It's all in your body language! The way you move and hold your body, the gestures you make, your facial expressions and tone of voice – pretty much everything aside from what you say – speaks volumes to other people.

As social creatures, we're tuned into other people's non-verbal communication. We instinctively know what it means if someone won't make eye contact (shy or has something to hide); if they look down at their feet the whole time (lacking in confidence); if they speak in whispers (the same) or if they smile but it doesn't meet their eyes (insincere).

The good news is that, with some work and a lot of practice, you can tailor your body language to make it work for you, to let it tell the story that you want other people to see. To portray yourself as confident even if you're still trembling inside.

The real beauty of this is that, as well as convincing other people, studies show that adopting a certain form of body language helps you to feel whatever emotion naturally goes along with it too. In short, you can also convince yourself. More on that soon.

But for now, let's look at what sort of body language demonstrates confidence?

Think back for a moment to chapter three and our discussion of default communication styles. Can you remember the typical body language used by confident, assertive people? Don't worry if you can't remember it all – I'm about to go over it again now. The ways that your body language can project confidence – in other words, assertive body language.

The Body Language of a Confident, Assertive Person

You portray yourself as confident when you:

- **Look people in the eye** – Being unable to make eye contact suggests you have something to hide, and people instinctively find it hard to trust you. Aim for eye contact about 60% of the time. It's also important to make sure the eye contact isn't aggressive. Michael Ellsberg, in his book, The Power of Eye Contact, says that *"in order for eye contact to feel good, one person cannot impose his visual will on another; it is a shared experience."*

- **Stand tall and hold yourself upright** – BUT relax your shoulders. Imagine a string running through your body pulling you up. *"[This] is a posture that projects confidence, not insecurity,"* says Pachter, *'You are open to the person to whom you are talking. And you can stand tall, regardless of your height."*

- **Walk with purpose** – no shuffling about, know your direction. Confident people also take longer steps.

- **Breathe normally** – don't hold your breath.

- **Talk at a normal volume** – no yelling or whispering, speak clearly and firmly, don't use an apologetic tone of voice. Try not to talk in 'questions' or sound as if you're asking questions when you're not.

- **Keep your facial expressions open** – and use them to illustrate your point.

- **Know what your hands are saying** – Make sure not to use aggressive or submissive hand gestures. An open hand, palm up, will communicate openness, cooperation, and acceptance. In contrast, crossing your arms indicates defensiveness.

- **Avoid fidgeting** – or the little things you usually do to release nervous tension, such as playing with your phone or picking your nails.

- **Offer a firm handshake** – a tell–tale sign of confidence. Practice it if you need to.

- **SMILE** – Don't grimace, just try for a relaxed smile.

- **Lean forward** – Leaning forward during a conversation indicates interest in the topic and the person sitting opposite you. Maintaining distance makes you look aloof.

- **Go for slow movements** – Fast movements make you look anxious or nervous.

QUICK TIP: If these things don't come naturally to you, practice them in front of a mirror. Pay attention too to your tone of voice and practice the way you sound.

My Own Top Tips ....
Anchoring
Here's a question for you. If you're faking it, how can you keep it up all day? How can you project confidence for a full 12 hours? A few minutes or throughout a meeting is possible but how do you maintain it, surely it will be exhausting?

Here's a little tip I like to share with my friends and clients

– anchor your self-confident pose to something you see often throughout the day. It could be as simple as a doorway, or the water cooler. Each time you pass through the doorway or walk past the water cooler, make it a point to check your body language. Is your spine straight? Is your head up, with your shoulders back? Are you smiling? Make the adjustments needed each time you walk through the doorway or spot the water cooler, and you'll be able to maintain confident body language all day.

Acting 'As If'
Body language hacks aside, here's another trick to convince people of your self-confidence – it's called acting 'as if'. You act 'as if' you're already the supremely confident person you want to be. Each time you aren't sure of how to act, think 'what would someone who is really confident do?' and do the same.

It may feel forced at first but the more you do it – and the more positive feedback you receive as people assume it's authentic – the easier it will become. Soon, you won't be acting anymore.

Real Life Case Study – Jane

Jane, 23, graduated from university and completed a post-graduate course in communications. Faking it until she made it worked for her.

She says: *"All of my life, I was painfully shy. With strangers and even with friends, I struggled to communicate or to be assertive in any way. I think people found it very hard to deal with me. I had one close friend who I'd had since early childhood but I often feared that I* held her back with my shyness.

"Being shy was a torment for me, I so wanted to be confident and popular. It followed me all through my childhood and even through university. It held me back in so many ways. I was too scared to join groups, to mingle with other people, to enjoy my university years properly. I doubted that I could ever be confident enough to work at my chosen career. I wanted to change, but I didn't know how.

"Finally, I started my post-graduate studies and ended up sharing a house with six other people. The first night, I couldn't face sitting in a room with a bunch of strangers – trying to make small talk with people I didn't know was a terror of mine – so I panicked and suggested we go to the local bar.

"That one move seemed to signal confidence to my housemates; they thought that I was confident, can you believe it? So, I just pretended I was, and it spiraled from there. No-one knew me, there were no expectations, so I pretended to be someone I wasn't. Someone confident, someone who wasn't afraid of everyone and everything.

"It was only one night a few months later when I sat chatting to someone new that it dawned on me: I wasn't pretending anymore. I didn't need to. I really did feel more confident, and I didn't struggle with the shyness so much. Sure, I had the occasional unsure moment and when I did, I reverted to faking it again but those moments were few and far between.

"Now, I don't think anything of talking to new people, of ordering at the bar, or mingling at events. It came naturally to me because I'd already been doing it (albeit faking it) for *months anyway.*

"If only someone had told me that faking it, or pretending, could actually help me overcome my shyness and feel more confident, I would have tried it years ago!"

Not Sure You Want to Fake It?
You may be reading this and thinking, *'but I don't want to fake it/I don't want to deceive/I just want to be me',* and that's completely understandable. The term 'faking it' goes against nearly all advice you've ever been given to just be yourself. But how about we change the language a bit. Instead of calling it 'faking it', think of yourself as conducting an experiment.

You are carrying out a social science experiment to see how people's attitudes towards you – and your own attitude in return – can change when you portray yourself as more confident. Give it a week and watch the results. I guarantee you'll be so impressed you'll want to continue the experiment.

Here's another important point to remember too: it's not deception to want to improve yourself. What could be more genuine than a sincere attempt to better yourself and become more confident?

It's Scientifically Proven…
I mentioned earlier that using confident body language can improve your own confidence too, and it's true. There's science to prove it. Let's look at some examples…

How Posture Influences Self-Confidence, Mood and Neurochemistry

Research shows that your posture can influence how you feel about yourself. A study at Ohio State University asked 71 student participants to either sit up straight (confident posture) or to slouch with their face looking at their knees (doubtful posture). All 71 were then asked to write down their best or worst qualities.

The participants then completed a self-evaluation and identified how likely they were to believe the things they wrote about themselves according to their posture. The results were striking.

Those students in the confident posture were much more likely to believe whatever they wrote down, demonstrating considerably more confidence in their thoughts than those who sat in the doubtful posture. *"Their confident, upright posture gave them more confidence in their own thoughts, whether they were positive or negative,"* says Richard Petty, co-author of the study and professor of psychology at the university. *"People assume their confidence is coming from their own thoughts. They don't realize their posture is affecting how much they believe in what they're thinking."* He added: *"Sitting up straight is something you can train yourself to do, and it has psychological benefits – as long as you generally have positive thoughts."* Also proving how important our chapter on getting the right, positive mindset is in order to become a confident and assertive woman.

Other studies have found similar correlations between self-confidence and posture. Researchers from Columbia and Stanford, for instance, discovered that using *'powerful postures'* – i.e., expansive and open postures – boosts testosterone and reduces levels of the stress hormone, cortisol. This combination is associated with positive results.

Further studies at Berkeley and Harvard also discovered that people who adopted powerful postures took risks they probably wouldn't otherwise have taken, increasing their own self-confidence by assuming postures they interpret as confident. A great example of acting 'as if'.

Grin and Bear It: Reduce Stress Fast

You've no doubt heard the phrase *'grin and bear it'* but probably didn't know that smiling – even when you don't feel like it – can have beneficial psychological effects.

A study by the University of Kansas sought to test this theory by having participants smile while completing stressful tasks. Participants were asked to place chopsticks in their mouths in certain ways to recreate either a neutral expression, a standard smile (using the muscles around the mouth only) or a Duchenne smile (uses both the muscles around the mouth and eyes). Only half the participants were instructed to smile, so using the chopsticks tested whether physically smiling (without intending to) would still have the same benefit.

The study proved smiling influences both our psychological and physical state. Participants who were instructed to smile, especially those with the Duchenne smile, had lower heart rates after the stressful activity than those who held a neutral expression.

Likewise, those with chopsticks forcing them to smile (but

who were not expressly told to smile) also reported feeling some positive benefit, greater than those with neutral expressions.

In short, smiling during brief stressful moments can reduce the body's response to stress, regardless of whether you feel happy or not.

"The next time you are stuck in traffic or are experiencing some other type of stress," says psychological scientist Sarah Pressman, co-author of the study, "you might try to hold your face in a smile for a moment. Not only will it help you 'grin and bear it' psychologically, but it might actually help your heart health as well!"

How Does It Work?
You're probably wondering how on earth your body posture, smiling or other body languages can influence your physical and psychological health. It almost sounds too incredible to be true, doesn't it? Especially considering that sometime you may be faking, as well.

But you see, your body and brain are talking to one another constantly, and it's a two-way street of communication. Your body language reflects the thoughts and feelings in your mind but at the same time, your thoughts and feelings are influenced by the messages your body language sends to the brain. Adopting positive body language, therefore, can send your brain the message that you are a more confident person.

Take the notion of smiling even if you're not happy. The brain receives messages from your mouth that you are smiling, therefore it determines that you should be in a positive mood – and makes sure that you are. That's why putting a pencil lengthwise between your teeth when reading a comic – triggering a smile – makes you find the comic strip funny.

Your brain constantly receives messages from all over your body helping it to determine how you should be feeling. So, standing up tall, shoulders back, spine straight, in a confident pose, tells your brain that you are feeling confident (even if you're not) and it reciprocates.

Walking forcefully too can boost your self-confidence. Adopt the posture above and walk with purposeful strides, making each stride a little longer than normal.

I mentioned adopting the *'power pose'* for an immediate confidence boost. If you're a fan of Grey's Anatomy, you will have seen Amelia Shepherd take a moment before surgeries to stand feet apart with her hands on her hips. That's a reflection of how strong your pose can make you feel.

An alternative power pose is to stand feet apart again with knees bent a little and hands above your head. Adopt a big cheesy smile, look up and inhale deeply. As you inhale, reach up and try to touch the ceiling. Hold the pose for a minute at a time, and you will send the message to your brain that you feel strong, powerful and confident. This is ideal for before a job interview, date or any situation where you need a strong and confident state of mind.

I hope by now that you have some appreciation of how effective body language can be, not only in convincing other people of what you want them to believe but also in convincing yourself too.

There's no shame in acting 'as if' or faking it if you need to in the short term; everyone does it.

Most people don't come out of the box (or the womb!) supremely confident; it's a job of work.

Indeed, even the most confident person can have crises now and again, or face challenges outside of their comfort zone. When that happens, what do they do? They put their chin up, head held high, shoulders back… and pretend. Pretend that it doesn't faze them, that they aren't secretly terrified by what they're facing, or overwhelmed by it. That's another version of acting 'as if'.
And isn't our brain fascinating? It's so flexible that faking it helps us to make it. So, why wouldn't you give it a go?!

Chapter 8 – Taking Risks, Seeking Courage, Finding Confidence

"Don't ever make decisions based on fear. Make decisions based on hope and possibility. Make decisions based on what should happen, not what shouldn't."
Michelle Obama

How Fear Can Hold Us Back

Before we move on to talk about being assertive in specific contexts and environments – such as at work, in interviews, at home, and with friends – I want to take this opportunity to talk about fear. Or more specifically, about finding the courage to face your fears.

Often the reason we lack self-confidence or fail to be assertive is that we're afraid… perhaps scared of how people will react or worried that we're not strong enough/brave enough/clever enough/popular enough/[insert your own fear here]. Sometimes these fears are imagined or are worries caused by real disturbing past experiences. Either way, they have the same effect on our fear.

It's worth taking some time to try to ascertain exactly what you're fearful of and to create a plan to address it. Actively changing your behavior can help you feel more confident.

How to Identify your Fears

Determine your specific fears. Write a list of what scares you; it may be things you've never even thought about before. Be warned: this might not be an easy process.

Once you have identified your fear(s), try to identify the root cause. Are there any specific experiences that may have contributed to the fear? If so, think of positive experiences to offset the negative. If you fear standing up for yourself at work, for instance, because you once had a bad experience when you did so, think now of all the times when you managed to do it without negative consequences.

If you cannot identify a cause of your fear, it's more likely to be a social fear, such as fear of failure, or a fear borne of a memory. In this case, try to think of times when doing the thing you fear did not manifest in a bad experience. You may also find that acknowledging your fears could be the first step to overcoming them.

As well as acknowledging your fear and worry, take some time to recognize your courage in other situations as well. Everyone is courageous in some way – you may fear public speaking, for instance, but perhaps you've recently moved to a different part of the country or another country entirely for a new job or a new start. That takes courage too.

Recognizing your own courage will encourage you to appreciate that your timidity in certain situations doesn't have to be set in stone; you do have the courage inside to change it.

Finally, create a plan to build courage. You can do so by using some of the behaviors designed to build courage I mention below.

Behaviors to Build Courage Fast

There are some recognized techniques to build courage and reduce fear. Before I talk about context-specific ways of boosting assertiveness, allow me to highlight some of these methods here. You can then tailor them to your personal situation.

"You gain strength, courage, and confidence by every experience in which you really stop to look fear in the face. You are able to say to yourself, 'I have lived through this horror. I can take the next thing that comes along.' You must do the thing you think you cannot do."
Eleanor Roosevelt

Scripting
As the name implies, scripting is a form of rehearsal… where you think about everything you might want to say during an event or interaction and conceptualize or create a 'script' for it in your head (or on paper if necessary). Research the people you will be talking to or the situation you might find yourself in and create a dialogue of questions and answers that can steer you through the discussion.

Consider role-playing with a friend or colleague ahead of time for practice too. Having a script and a game plan in mind will help you feel calm and more confident. Repetition is also useful – practice makes perfect, as they say.

I have personally used scripting numerous times ahead of important job interviews. Before I've gone in there, I've known exactly what I want to say, how to get my best self across, and have been prepared for a host of questions from the interviewer. Of course, there are some interview questions that still come from left field but knowing that you already have the answers to most of the likely questions helps instill confidence and take the nerves out of the situation.

In case you're wondering, I'd say I got the job 8 or 9 times out of 10. Scripting really works!

Framing
Framing is a behavioral technique that helps to take the sting out of big intimidating situations by making them seem commonplace or banal. If you suffer performance anxiety in exams, for instance, you can reframe the experience by calling it a 'quiz' instead of a scary 'examination'.

Likewise, if you typically freeze during job interviews, you can reframe it to consider it a 'little chat' instead. Framing can help shape how you think and feel about a situation and reduce or eliminate the anxiety you feel ahead of them.

Take MMA fighters, a great example of the psychological power of framing. Ahead of a cage fight, MMA fighters typically frame the fights as either another day at the gym, a job to do, or a valuable learning experience. With the latter approach, win or lose doesn't matter – it's a valuable chance to learn. Athletes hone their performances by taking the same approach. Use these three approaches to any intimidating situation and avoid psyching yourself out ahead of time.

Stop Comparisons
It sounds simple but comparing yourself to others is counterproductive and can hamper your self-confidence. Other people are bound to be courageous in ways that you are not; you're just as likely to have courage in areas that they do not. Some people, too, project courage in order to intimidate or to hide their own insecurities.

Remember that you never truly know what is going on in someone else's life or psyche. We all know someone who seems so put-together that they put us to shame but chances are that they envy us in some way too.

The only way to genuinely boost your self-confidence is to focus on yourself. Put the energy you typically spend comparing yourself to others towards yourself; don't waste it on pointless comparisons. If you do find yourself falling down the comparison rabbit hole, take the time to remind yourself of all the courageous things you do in other ways.

Progressive Desensitization
When you're identifying your fear, it may become apparent that you won't be able to tackle or overcome it all in one go. That's where progressive desensitization comes in… it's a technique whereby you expose yourself to small, incremental amounts of the thing you fear the most. The idea is to then become comfortable with it stage by stage.

This is a favored way of approaching phobias, such as a fear of spiders. Imagine this is your fear – you'd start by viewing a spider in a box, safely contained away from you. Once your heart stops racing, maybe after 30 minutes, take the next step – perhaps opening the lid while someone else makes sure the spider doesn't escape, and so on and so forth.

Alternatively, consider the fear of public speaking. Perhaps you have a new job that requires you to give regular presentations to the rest of the company but you break out in a cold sweat whenever you think of it.

Using a scale, say your fear of public speaking is a 10, you might want to start by acclimatizing yourself to smaller related fears that are 5 or 6 on the scale. It might be that your 5 is a reluctance to speak up in a small group, so try it in an informal gathering first. Once you do that, aim for a 6 – speaking up in a formal meeting. Aim to become comfortable with these smaller challenges until they slip down to a 2 or 3 on the anxiety scale.

The next step is to move on to your new 5s or 6s; these will more than likely be the fears that were 9 or 10 on the scale before. Say standing in front of a small group of your colleagues and giving a pre-prepared presentation. Once you feel comfortable with that, then giving a presentation to the entire company is no longer quite the terrifying feat it once was.

That's successful desensitization and if you're determined to tackle your fears, it can be a very successful strategy. Be warned that it does require determination and perseverance, of course, and, in the case of public speaking above, may well need you to seek out opportunities to reduce your fears.

The good thing is that such baby steps can be used for any endeavor.

Develop A Courage Habit
A lack of courage is often an influencing factor in many shattered dreams. The number of times I've heard people say they'd love to start their own business or move abroad or do a hundred different things that scare them. Unfortunately, in many cases, people allow their fears or lack of courage – often masquerading as procrastination or perfectionism or Imposter Syndrome – to stop them from reaching for the stars.

So, how can you develop courage and flow with the fear, as opposed to letting it paralyze you?

Courage allows you to take action in the face of fear, even if it's imperfect, and develop the ability to bounce back when faced with setbacks. It's a very powerful skill to learn.

Life coach Kate Swoboda believes courage can be created by small daily actions – hence the courage habit. Swoboda, author of The Courage Habit: How to Accept Your Fears, Release the Past, and Live Your Courageous Life, says: *"What if our fear-based behaviors were more habits than anything else? ...If fear-based behaviors were habits, then the good news was that these habits could be changed and we didn't need to be stuck in them, forever."*

In her book, she argues that ignoring fear only works in the short-term; in the long term, it's exhausting to pretend you're not afraid. Fighting it or trying to silence it doesn't work, either; by doing so, we 'abuse' ourselves. So, we should recognize that fear is a normal emotion and learn how to use it, rather than try to ignore or placate it.

Taking small steps every day to boost your courage can help you adopt the courage habit.

Why Taking Risks Is a Good Thing
Do you know what most of the very successful people in life have in common? They have failed.... more than once. Often over and over again.

That's because they are not afraid to challenge themselves and take risks. Correction: they may be afraid but they do it anyway. They know that remaining in their comfort zone isn't the way to achieve success. After all, if you don't take risks, not only does your courage never grow but your comfort zone shrinks.

The best way to boost your self-confidence is to open yourself up to new experiences and take risks – and allow yourself to fail.

Here's why failure isn't necessarily a bad thing… it can teach us a heck of a lot. If we see failures as opportunities to learn and improve, we turn a negative into a positive. And it's suddenly not so intimidating anymore.

The Harry Potter series of books is one of the most popular ever, and yet author JK Rowling was turned down by no less than 12 publishers. Imagine if she'd seen the failures as the end of the story!

Thankfully she didn't and, together with 'Harry', she changed the face of the publishing industry. More than 500 million books have since been sold worldwide in 80 different languages.

According to the Pottermore website, this means that on average 1 in 15 people in the world own a Harry Potter book. I do, I have the whole collection. I'm grateful JK Rowling didn't put her pen down/close her laptop after her 1st, 2nd, 3rd or even 11th rejection.

Take heart from this: in order to expand your lifestyle, comfort zone, courage and confidence, put yourself out there and try. Try something new, do something that scares you, and consider potential failure a chance to learn and an opportunity to build character.

Arguably one of America's best Presidents, Abraham Lincoln, lost eight elections and failed in business twice (not to mention had a nervous breakdown) before he was finally elected to High Office. It's altogether possible that he was only able to lead the country through such hard times because of his experience of failure.

Take a risk, embrace failure and eventually, you will succeed… and your self-confidence will skyrocket as a result.

Assertiveness in Context & Environment

I've talked a lot in this book about the likely causes for a lack of confidence and the reasons many women struggle to be assertive. I've also shared behavioral tips with you on how to build courage, tackle your fears and become more confident.

Now is the time to put it all into context.

The final part of this book discusses assertiveness in various different environments – such as how to be assertive at work (examines when it's appropriate and how best to achieve it), at home with family, friends and acquaintances, and how to handle typically awkward situations, such as when giving or receiving compliments or criticism.

This chapter, in particular, discusses the issue of assertiveness at work, whether you're the boss, a worker or middle management.

Chapter 9 – Assertiveness in the Workplace

Why It's So Important
As we have established, assertiveness is one of the most important skills to learn in order to be effective, successful and respected in and out of the workplace. Learning how to say 'no', for instance, can mean the difference between a satisfying work-life balance or one that destroys your mental (and physical) health.

Many people worry that being assertive could adversely affect their career, so they bite back any protests or keep their opinions to themselves. All too often employees assume employers don't want confident, outspoken members of staff but it's not the truth. Confident employers welcome feedback, good or bad. Recruiters too say statistics show that individuality, assertiveness, and free-thinking is prized in an employee.

There are indeed times to be vocal but how do you know when that is? Many people, particularly if they are new to leadership, struggle to know when to use their assertiveness. Leaders need confidence and assertiveness in spades but as we already know, being too aggressive is counterproductive.

Being The Boss: When To Be Assertive With Your Team
So, when is the best time to be assertive with your team? You may be the leader but that doesn't mean you have all the answers. You do know, however, that leading assertively and respecting your team is the key to success.

But do you need to be assertive with your team all the

time?

Not necessarily; indeed, knowing when to assert yourself and when to hold back is a key skill to learn.

So, let's have a look at the sort of situations where it pays to be assertive with your team…

To Boost Morale
If morale is low in your team – it happens! – you'll need to use all of the skills available to you to motivate the team out of the slump. Being passive and accepting the status quo will only ensure the problem continues. Likewise, issuing orders and being aggressive with people will simply foster resentment at a time when you need everyone to work together.

You'll need to be assertive in order to spark passion and morale in your team. You can do this by:

- Giving everyone the chance to talk (not just the usual suspects)
- Assigning different responsibilities to team members
- Encouraging the team to experiment with different solutions (allowing them to take ownership of a project)
- By being positive
- Sharing your opinions with your team and listening to them.
- In short, by setting a good example.

Tackling Difficult Employees
When you're the boss, there's a lot of responsibility on your shoulders. Not only do you need to ensure the team works productively but you may have to manage other

people's expectations and strong personalities at times. Conflict resolution certainly requires assertiveness, if it is to have a positive outcome (read on for more). However, often there are numerous smaller personnel-related issues that you may have to deal with first.

You may have to flex your assertiveness muscle in order to keep people in check. Perhaps you have an employee or team member who is persistently late, or whose work is sloppy. What do you do? You have several choices here.

Do you try to ignore it, and hope it improves? Quick tip – This is NEVER a good idea as it very rarely improves by itself, and you run the risk of frustrating other team members who witness your inactivity and resent covering for their slack colleague. Being aggressive and belittling the employee in front of everyone else is a negative approach too, and only serves to lose your respect among the rest of the team.

Instead, a better choice is to handle it privately, sit down and discuss their behavior. Being assertive doesn't mean you need to be confrontational. Start by explaining why their behavior isn't appropriate but give them the chance to speak. Perhaps your instructions weren't clear; there was some sort of misunderstanding; your team member is struggling with something at home that is affecting his or her work. If so, you may be able to work together to resolve the issues. Weekly check-ins may also help.

You may need to escalate things if your attempts to deal with the problem have been unsuccessful, which means you must be firm, though still respectful. This is actually a good lesson to learn: even being assertive doesn't always solve the problem, and you may need to escalate it further.

Conflict Resolution

Many of us spend more time with our coworkers than we do with family, friends and maybe even our significant other. It stands to reason that occasional conflicts will crop up as colleagues argue, disagree, fall out and even experience professional jealousy. This can harm team morale if it isn't handled carefully – and assertively. An assertive leader steps in early to try to resolve potential conflicts before it gets out of control.

You could opt for the traditional idea of conflict resolution – getting the two involved parties in one room and listening to both sides of the issue. You may then decide the two employees can't sit next to one another and move them to different parts of the office or assign them to different teams. If one is acting inappropriately, you will need to handle this head-on and explain why it is unacceptable.

I've personally found what I believe is a much better form of conflict resolution – one passed on to me by my mentor – is to encourage both parties to take responsibility for dealing with the issue. This still takes considerable confidence and assertiveness from you to pull off. And it tends to work better when grievances between team members are work-led, rather than personality-led.

In this case, you invite both parties into a private room, as before, but instead of simply listening to their grievances, you invite them to listen to one another. The important thing in this sort of conflict resolution is to explain that both sides need to remain calm and civil but can use this time to examine and explain the issues they have with each other. Taking it in turns, the one not speaking listens and then addresses the concerns that have been raised.

I have found that it's important to inform both parties that each is important to the team, the meeting will not be an attack, and that they shouldn't necessarily apologize for something they do not believe they have done. However, if they listen calmly and put themselves in the other person's shoes, they may realize that their behavior could have been better, in which case it is helpful to acknowledge it as such. (This helps to take the pressure off somewhat and encourages a calmer evaluation of the meeting).

During the meeting, you will need to be on hand to ensure discussions stay on track, are productive and don't veer into blame territory or deteriorate into an argument.

Quick tip – Evaluate the potential players in this meeting first to see if this sort of conflict resolution is suitable. It's important to give everyone the chance to have their say but some people will not want to discuss the issue in front of the other person or may lack the confidence to state the problem upfront. They too may struggle with being assertive enough to say what is troubling them.

Note too, that this sort of conflict resolution may not be appropriate for certain sensitive situations, such as bullying (where one party may be too intimidated), and official procedures should be followed in cases of sexual harassment or legally sensitive concerns.

An office junior I once worked with a long time ago was bullied terribly by our shared boss. As a co-worker seeing this (and senior to her), I raised it officially with the manager of the department. We both attended a meeting where she was given the opportunity to state her case, even without the other person present, and… she refused to say a single word. She was too scared/shy. Instead, she let me do the talking for her, and thankfully, the issue was addressed.

Had it been solely up to her, however, the bullying may well have continued.

Real Life Case Study – Emma

Emma, an employee in a London PR firm, took part in a similar form of conflict resolution with her immediate boss, Roland.

"Everything was fine when the owner of the company was in the office but as soon as she left, Roland turned into a different person. He was pushy, bossy and often unwarrantedly critical of me. I am a professional, so I felt it wasn't necessary." says Emma.

To address Emma's grievances, the owner of the company sat her and Roland down and held a 'state of the Union' meeting, where Emma got her chance to explain the issue she had. "When I said I felt victimized, Roland apologized for making me feel that way but stood by his role in the office when the boss was away. And even though he didn't admit to any actual wrongdoing, I felt a lot better after the meeting. It felt like we'd sorted a lot of things out and I had been listened to.

"Things improved after that as well, and I could tell that Roland was more conscious of the way he behaved towards people as a result, which made me happier. To be honest, after that I didn't have any complaints, and while it took quite a lot of courage for me to speak up, I'm very glad I did. I feel more confident about things as a result."

Emma's response demonstrates how well meetings like this can work to empower your team while also providing a good technique for conflict resolution.

Techniques For Being An Assertive Boss

If you struggle to be assertive as the boss, it's worth learning a couple of techniques to help you stand tall. I've already suggested a few in our last chapters such as scripting and framing, but as a general rule:

- **Believe in yourself** – You are a valued member of your team and company.

- **Set boundaries** – and be clear about them. Employees are not mind readers. Clearly define what you expect and what you refuse to tolerate.

- **Control your Emotions** – As a leader, you will be tasked with dealing with some highly charged situations, and it's crucial that you control your emotions. Getting angry, frustrated or upset doesn't set a calming tone or a good example. If you feel emotion overcome you, take a break.

- **Speak in 'I' statements** – We're going to talk more about those in our next chapter, but needless to say, you should speak in the first person when you address your team. That way they will understand that you are expressing your own feelings and less likely to feel like you are blaming them.

- **Address issues directly** – don't allow them to fester or for staff to gossip about each other. Hold people accountable, and don't let poor employees get away with inappropriate behavior or sloppy work.

- **Watch your body language** – Think back to chapter seven and use some of the confident body language tips I shared.

- **Learn to say 'no' when appropriate** – You can't always agree to everything your team wants, and it's important to say no when you need to. That goes for members of your team too: don't be surprised if you hear the word 'no' now and again too.

When and How To Be Assertive with Anyone

What if you're not the boss? When is it appropriate for you to be assertive in the office or at work? A lot of people think the best way to be successful at work is not to rock the boat but there are certain times or situations where you'd be advised to speak out.

They include:

- **When instinct suggests something is wrong** – Don't ignore it, even if other people do. If you believe there's a problem with a client, for instance, speak up and warn others. You may regret it if you don't. Even if the powers that be reject your opinions, at least you've made sure your voice is heard.

- **If you can't do something** – Taking on challenges is a good way to develop new skills but if you take on too much, or are asked to do something that you genuinely do not have the skills to do, you need to speak out. Say no or ask for help. Either way is better than promising something you cannot deliver. The same is true when you don't have the time to complete the work too. Perhaps you already have two big assignments on, and your boss wants to give you a third. Consider if it's even possible and if it isn't, say no or ask your manager which is the most important to finish first.

- **If it goes against your ethics** – Sometimes we're asked to do certain things at work that may go against our personal morals or ethics – such as promoting a product that you don't believe in. You may consider it necessary to ignore your instincts in certain cases in order to do your job well but there may also be times when you can't compromise any further. In such cases, speak up and be honest. You will earn the respect of your colleagues and employers, and they will appreciate knowing where you stand.

- **If it threatens your safety** – If there are any situations which threaten your safety at work, you need to step back and look at the situation carefully. Avoid rushing as that's a typical cause of workplace accidents. If there is no emergency element to the request (and perhaps even if there is), you may want to politely but firmly state that you are not willing to risk your safety and turn the work down.

How To Be An Assertive Employee At Work

We've covered the when but what about the how? How can you be more assertive? As well as the framing, scripting and other ideas I covered earlier, here are a few more recommendations:

- **Change your verbs** – In order to send a clear message and be more definite when you communicate, consider the language you use. In particular, the verbs you use. Instead of 'should, could, or need to', for instance, choose 'will, want, choose to'. Let's do a test and see which sounds the most emphatic…'I should be taking the day off work next week' versus 'I will be taking the day off work next week'. Or, 'I could do the training course' versus 'I want to do the training course'

The second version is much stronger, isn't it, and leaves less room for debate or negotiation. After all, you don't want the boss reacting to 'I should be taking the day off work next week' by saying 'Well if it's not that important, can you make it the following week and do this work instead?'

Other language that devalues your assertiveness is 'just', such as 'I just thought'… it suggests that what comes next isn't really important. Likewise, phrases such as 'I might be wrong but…' doesn't do anything for your assertiveness either. Ditto, ending your sentences with a raised voice that seems to indicate a question doesn't fill people with confidence.

- **Ask for extra time** – Sometimes you can't think what to say to a request straightaway or you may be too emotional to handle it. You might also want to evaluate the pros and cons before making your decision either way. In such cases, don't feel intimidated or driven to reply immediately. Simply ask for more time (and don't apologize for doing so). You could say something like 'Your request has caught me by surprise, I'll get back to you in 10 minutes.'

- **Set your boundaries** – You don't necessarily have to inform other people of your boundaries but knowing what you will and will not allow enables you to stay firm and empower you to say yes or no when you need to. You don't want to be a bully but neither do you want to allow other people to walk all over you. If you do have to say no, be direct and don't hesitate. If you feel an explanation is needed, keep it brief.

- **Use the assertiveness LADDER** – Here's a useful assertiveness mnemonic to use whenever you struggle to express yourself or face a particular problem you need to fix – LADDER. Write one or two sentences for each step on the ladder, practice your steps alone and then put it into practice in reality.

LADDER stands for...

- **L – Look at your rights:** Everyone has the right to be heard, respected and safe in the workplace. Remind yourself of your rights and it will give you more confidence.
- **A – Arrange a meeting:** It's not always possible to be assertive in the moment, so arrange a meeting to discuss the issue properly. Obviously, this step may not be relevant to all situations, so can be skipped if necessary.
- **D – Define the problem**: Write down the facts, avoid using emotional language and be very clear so the other person fully understands your position. The other person may not even know what the problem is, so be sure to fully define it for them.
- **D – Describe your feelings:** Once you have presented the facts, describe how you are feeling, using 'I' statements only and avoiding placing blame (such as 'I am frustrated' rather than 'You frustrate me'). This will help the other person to appreciate your viewpoint.
- **E – Express your needs/wants:** Have a short want or need statement ready that sums up what you want from the meeting. Be brief, to the point and firm. If you can, include a solution, albeit recognize that it may need to be fine-tuned once the other person has had their say. Be specific

too – if, for instance, you want to ask for more flexibility at work, have a solution in mind demonstrating exactly what that would be. Perhaps it's to be able to arrive 30 minutes later or to leave an hour earlier. Prove how you will make up that time by working from home.
- **R – Reinforce the benefits:** Using positive language, reinforce the mutual benefits for both sides in coming to a solution. Frame it as a win-win for both parties.

Keeping Safe: Dealing With Sexual Harassment At Work

Before I move on to talking about assertiveness in interviews, I want to briefly touch on a work-related topic that affects us all and discuss how you can handle it if it is happening to you… sexual harassment at work.

We'd no doubt like to think that the working world is more enlightened nowadays, but nearly a third of U.S. women (three in 10) have suffered from unwanted or inappropriate sexual advances from co-workers, according to an ABC News-Washington Post poll. A quarter of those was from people who were in senior positions to them at work.

Of those subjected to unwanted advances, 8 in 10 said it rose to sexual harassment, while a third said it went further to sexual abuse. That's about 47 million women in the U.S. who have either been sexually harassed or sexually abused at work. Incredible, isn't it?

Even worse is the lack of action taken. Nearly all the women questioned (95%) who personally experienced sexual harassment said male harassers are usually not punished. Which goes some way to explaining why less than half of victims (42%) reported it to a supervisor.

Consequences for the female victims, however, can be severe. 83% of women report being angry about it, 64% intimidated and 52% humiliated.

The statistics across the pond in the UK make similarly grim reading. According to a BBC survey for BBC Radio 5 Live, half of women (53%) and a fifth of men have been sexually harassed at work. Incidents ranged from sexual assaults to inappropriate comments, with a quarter of people suffering inappropriate banter or jokes, while 1 in 7 suffered from inappropriate touching. A third of women victims were targeted by a senior manager or boss. As in the U.S., 63% didn't report it to anyone.

Of the 20% of women who did report it, 80% reported that nothing changed and 16% said the situation actually got worse afterward, according to a report by the TUC.

With such harassment so prevalent, it's important you know your rights – and be confident enough to assert them – should it ever happen to you.

Recognize & Act
Every case of sexual harassment is different and the exact approach to take will depend on your personal situation. Sexual harassment may include unwanted sexual advances and requests for sexual favors, or some form of physical, verbal or visual harassment at work. It can be carried out by a supervisor, boss, co-worker or even someone who doesn't work at your company such as a client or customer (assuming the employer knows about the conduct and doesn't take steps to solve the problem.)

Generally, sexual harassment comes in two main forms:

- Creating a hostile working environment as a result of the harassment.
- Or quid-pro-quo harassment – when a benefit to the employee is implied, stated or implicit if they submit to an unwelcome sexual advance first.

So, how can you handle it if it happens to you?

1. **Speak Up:** If something makes you uncomfortable – whether it's behavior, jokes or banter – speak up. State the behavior is unacceptable and insist it stops. Legally, for such behavior to be classed as sexual harassment, it must be 'unwelcome', so don't ignore it and hope it stops. Likewise, refuse all invitations outside of work, don't flirt back or send mixed signals. Direct communication is key, so say **NO**.

   Communicate immediately that the behavior is unwelcome. You could say something like, 'Your behavior is making me uncomfortable, please stop'. It may be enough to make the other person stop. So too may threatening to report them. If it doesn't stop, however, you will need to take further action.

2. **Write it all down:** Ideally on a home computer, personal device or in a dated journal. Write down all details of the harassment, including dates, times and locations, and the names of any witnesses (you may want to ask witnesses to make a written account of the incident as well). Remember that others may read your notes later, so keep it objective and accurate. It's not a diary. Keep it where it is secure and can be easily accessed.

3. **Gather your records:** If you do take a claim forward, your harasser may try to defend themselves by making claims against your job performance. So, have all your work

records – performance reviews, emails, letters documenting your work, copies of your personnel file – to hand. Think of it as an active form of defense. If you do not have these things, try to gather them via legal means only. In some states, you are allowed to review your personnel file, and you should take copies if allowed, or write copious notes otherwise.

4. **Report the behavior:** As soon as any harassment starts, report it to your immediate supervisor and HR. For legal reasons, this is important as your employer needs to know about the conduct in order to be legally responsible for addressing it. Once informed, the company has the responsibility to address the misbehavior of co-workers, clients and customers alike.

    You can report it verbally but a formal letter is better (detailing the events and asking for a meeting, keep a copy of the letter for your records). Informing them either verbally or in writing should trigger the employer's responsibility to investigate. After reporting it to your supervisor, you may also want to report it to your Human Resources department if your company has one.

    Follow any official procedure the company has regarding sexual harassment to the letter.

    Important tip – If you do make a report to your supervisor and/or HR, keep a copy of everything you give your employer. If you fill in any company forms, ask to keep a copy for your records. If the employer refuses, tell them you will take a photograph of the form, and do so.

5. **Talk to others:** If it is safe for you to do so, talk to other women in your company. You may find they have been experiencing the abuse too. You can find allies this way.

Tell family, friends and supportive co-workers as well, as this may become evidence in any case later down the line.

6. **Escalate it:** If HR and/or your supervisor fail to respond to your complaint, report it to senior management. It's best to do so in a formal written letter, including any documentation regarding the incident.

Under Title VII of the Civil Rights Act of 1964 (in the U.S.), you cannot be punished for complaining about or filing a charge of sexual harassment. These Federal laws also protect you if you choose to join or testify on behalf of a co-worker experiencing harassment too. As always this is lay advice and if serious you may want to consult a Law Practitioner for advice before acting.

Assertiveness in Interviews

Before I close this chapter, I want to make a quick mention of another work-related issue, job interviews. Assertiveness is one of the most valuable character traits you can demonstrate in an interview. Employers value candidates who can be honest and confident in their abilities, and who aren't overwhelmed by the humility involved in the job-hunting process.

A little trick I like to use to help me stay confident in job interviews is to view it as a two-way conversation: just as they are interviewing you for a job, you are interviewing them to assess if it's a place you might want to work, and someone who you might want to work for. Such thinking helps to balance out the power dynamic.

Of course, interviews can still be nerve-wracking, so let me share a few tips for establishing confidence and demonstrating assertiveness while you are being quizzed ...

- **First impressions** – They start from the moment your interviewer sees you, so make a point of standing as soon as the interviewer approaches and reach out to shake his or her hand. Smile, make eye contact and hold your head up high with your back straight.

- **Sit across from the interviewer** – Assuming you are given the choice of seat, sitting across from the interviewer allows strong eye contact, enabling you to make a good connection. Remember, while eye contact is important, it shouldn't be overpowering. Glance away now and again!

- **Speak clearly and at a reasonable volume** – Assertiveness doesn't mean shouting. Use phrases too that suggests confidence, such as *'I know I can...'* or *'I'm confident I can...'* as opposed to tentative phrases like *'I believe I can.'*

- **Avoid the temptation to fidget** – If you are nervous, it's fine to mention it once, ideally with humor but then move on. Demonstrate that you can handle the circumstances with grace. When I interviewed people during job interviews, how well they performed under pressure gave me a useful indication of how well they could handle the stress of the job.

- **Ask questions throughout the interview** – Be assertive, ask about the company's future plans, how a typical day would look, opportunities for professional development, ask about the company's corporate style, etc.... This indicates your genuine interest in the job and shows you are a strong candidate. It also suggests that you would be committed to fitting in at the company and are already thinking of the role you will play there if hired.

- **Ensure your body language is open** – (don't cross your legs or arms) and mimic the assertive body language we talked about in chapter seven.

- **Remember at all times the difference between being aggressive and being assertive** – The latter respects the other party and demonstrates it via your communication. So, you can ask for what you want without making demands or say what you think without being impolite, for instance.

  It may also help you to know upfront what your 'bottom line' is, so you can understand what makes something a fair deal for you, and you know what you are prepared to negotiate. Assertiveness doesn't mean you get your own way all the time; expect negotiation and compromise. It will create a much better impression than an aggressive stance, or a passive one.

- **Share your ideas and be bold** – Know already how you intend to answer the obvious interview question, 'why should I hire you?' and be bold with your answer. Point out the benefits you will bring to the company and paint a picture. Mention too any likely challenges the company may have in the near future and offer your suggestions for how to successfully manage them.

  State your interest in the job if you truly want it, and don't leave the interview without either establishing the next steps or following up with a call to action.

Example Scenarios and Assertive Responses

Here's a couple of great examples of being assertive in an interview:

Showing more of what you have to offer:
Imagine your interviewer asks you questions that require specific detailed answers but doesn't allow you much chance to demonstrate what else you have to offer. An assertive person would answer the questions but also take the opportunity to expand upon their answers to provide more than the questions demand. The key, of course, is to make sure the extra information you provide relates specifically to the job description.

Be honest and relate other valid experiences:
The interviewer asks how you would handle a particular situation but you have no relevant experience of it to call upon. An assertive person wouldn't try to hide that lack of experience – it will be obvious on your resume anyway (and no doubt via your answer too). Instead, explain you do not have specific experience in that field but offer a probable answer based on common sense and logic.

Real Life Case Study – Rachel

Rachel, 35, lived in London and went for a job interview in New York for a very well-known and prestigious website. The job itself was to launch the UK arm of the American site, which she knew beforehand.

"It was a high-pressure situation" says Rachel. *"I flew to New York for two nights and interviewed with three different people from the company in that time, including*

the CEO. This would be a very high-profile launch from a flagship brand with lots of eyes on it. It had to be right.

"When I met the CEO, who had the final decision on any hiring, I presented my plan – complete with research, mock-ups, site plans and navigation suggestions, plus some observations about their potential British audience. In short, I gave him a dossier of launch plans, and while I acknowledged there was a lot I didn't yet know about the planned launch, I stressed that I was absolutely the best person to do it."

She grins. *"They could have thought I was incredibly cocky and hated it; thankfully, they appreciated the intent behind it, which was to show them how suitable I would be for the role."*

"It was the most work I'd ever done for an interview but they loved it. Ten minutes after I walked out of the meeting with the CEO, I got an ecstatic phone call from my recruitment agent to say I had the job. She was overwhelmed by how much they praised me. I must admit, I was too!"

Rachel's 'moxy' – or assertiveness to give it another name – paid off, and yours can too.

I hope this chapter has given you some ideas about how to be confident and assertive in the workplace and during interviews. It's no exaggeration to say that your future career success could hinge on how well you manage to adopt these skills and techniques into your work life.

Chapter 10 – Assertiveness Closer to Home

Assertiveness With Loved Ones

When we think of confidence and assertiveness, it's very easy to assume we only need it at work, or that it's only a problem if we lack it in our professional lives. And, of course, as I mentioned in my opening chapter, lacking confidence can put a dampener on your entire career trajectory if it's not tackled.

But, here's the thing: it can also negatively influence your life at home as well. Your relationship with your partner, your role amongst friends, your ability to make friends in the first place, if you can accept constructive criticism… it's all influenced by how well you can stand up for yourself.

If you're not happy at home, for instance, you certainly employ some of the assertive skills I've already taught you so far in this book to address it. They're transferable and they may just save your most important relationships. Likewise, children aren't the only ones swayed by negative influences and fake friends… strong self-confidence helps to ensure people won't take advantage of you.

Feel free to re-read the previous chapter with a view to any personal issues you may have rather than the professional. Putting a different hat on when revisiting chapter 9 may just help you find a solution that you can tailor to your home life too. That said, introducing such assertiveness techniques at home where emotions usually run highest can often feel like an even more difficult task.

If you're in the middle of a heated argument with your

spouse over whose turn it is to do the dishes, or upset that they forgot your birthday – again – or vehemently disagreeing over some element of child-rearing, you might struggle to remain calm. I'll be sharing some tips for how to establish appropriate communication with loved ones shortly in this chapter.

For now though, let me first ask you a more fundamental question: when is assertiveness appropriate?

Modern life tells us that we deserve it all: we should aim for the skies, shout our truths from the rooftops and take down anyone who gets in our way. That's what we're being lead to believe a strong modern-day woman is all about. But surely, it is better we take responsibility to do it in the right way and at the right time?

I will be the first to tell you should be confident, assertive and ambitious in life. In most cases, being assertive helps demonstrate self-confidence, personal dignity, and respect. You should always feel free to tell those around you that your needs matter and are important.

As we already know, passive people don't get their needs met and end up feeling misunderstood or frustrated. The same is true for aggressive people, of course. Assertiveness, therefore, seems to be the ideal middle ground BUT there are right and wrong ways to do it.

Remember, assertiveness = respect.

Let me paint a picture of instances that I would call *'assertiveness mistakes'*. Note, that I didn't call them failures. When you make a mistake, you haven't failed in your assertiveness you've just gained an opportunity to learn and grown. When you make an *'assertive mistake'* you may have just potentially used it in the wrong way, or at the wrong time, or when it wasn't even needed. You see, contrary to the impetus I mentioned earlier to *'take down anyone who gets in your way'*, things aren't always as cut and dried as that. Especially not with family.

Here's my first example: If you insist on your position and your views, for instance, without considering the other person's needs, wants and feelings, you may be perceived as self-righteous and aggressive and not as being assertive. Standing up for your position is one thing; standing up for your position as though it's the only reasonable one is another. The only response it tends to gain is either a defensive one or an attacking one.

The key to being truly assertive without being self-righteous or aggressive is to do it mindfully.

Mindful Assertiveness

You can avoid falling flat in your assertiveness by taking the other person's viewpoint into account; if you consider it open-mindedly it will probably feel just as legitimate as your own. That's mindful assertiveness in a nutshell. If you're not sure where the other person is coming from, ask them what they think or feel. Before you reply, try to at least imagine what could be going on with them.

Here's another question and one you should think about before responding to perceived slights: do you really need to justify yourself? Perhaps you can just agree to disagree, with friends especially, and acknowledging that your backgrounds/life experiences give you different but equally valid perspectives. If you do need to clarify your thoughts to the other party, consider how to do it in a way that is neither defensive nor self-righteous.

Finally, boost your own confidence by assuring yourself that no-one can invalidate your viewpoint, so you hardly need to go to battle over it.

Choose Battles Wisely
I find this point is key. I have a friend who will always argue with me over one fundamental point – whether or not God exists. I know, what sort of conversations are we having over a glass of wine, hey?!

I'm not going to go into detail over who believes in a Higher Power and who doesn't but needless to say, we disagree. After the topic popping up on a few occasions and having open discussions about it I feel that we're close enough friends to be able to respect each other and to see that each of us believe our view is valid. Fair enough right? – so let's agree to disagree.

Except for some reason, she can't ever leave it alone. Whenever she inevitably brings it up – and it invariably does at least a few times a year – she has to attack and belittle my views (she would probably consider it, 'educating'). I'm not even sure why, except for the fact that she seems to believe that in order to show her own viewpoints validity, she first has to try to shatter and undermine mine.

I'm made of hardier stuff than that and whilst I respect her enough to listen to her, it does not change my belief on the topic. The point is it doesn't really matter what the contentious issue is, neither person is ever going to change their view and hence bringing up the topic is just going into battle unnecessarily. The conflict is unwarranted, and, at times, I've even wondered if I want to remain friends with this person, even though she is a fantastic friend otherwise. Here's my tip: Don't fall into the same trap of being drawn into an unnecessary battle or argument. You can lose friends that way.

Being mindful in your assertiveness – considering the other person and the circumstance, and whether it's really crucial that you put your point across at all costs – will increase the chances of it being respectful. And, it should be pointed out, more effective for your continuing relationship. It's important to note that this is not giving in or allowing yourself to be walked over. It's just that when you choose to use your assertiveness, make sure it's over something worth being assertive about.

For instance, if have a close family member that leaves the toilet seat up at times, it's hardly something to blow out of proportion. There's probably no need to 'assert yourself' here. However, if they do it on a continual basis without consideration for others and the bare ceramic toilet bowl is freezing in the middle of the night, well, it might be worth comment. Something like, "Honey [endearment of your choice], could you put the toilet seat down when you finish at night. It's not very comfortable when I sit down in the dark and don't see that it's not down."

Hopefully, job done. Issue resolved. That surely beats passive-aggressively slamming the toilet seat down loudly at 4 am in the morning or hiding the toilet paper/throwing out the magazines in protest! (No matter how satisfying it may feel at the time ;)) If you continually follow the passive-aggressive path, things will inevitably become hostile.

Also, speak up straight away when issues occur; don't let

them fester. The exception is to take a breather if emotions are running high – more on that shortly.

It's all too easy to fall into a pattern of passive aggression in our personal lives, especially if you let problems develop and fail to address them. Frustrations grow and every small issue grows until it becomes a disaster or catastrophe, thus creating a hostile environment. Raising issues in a timely manner, instead, allows you to maintain control and keep mutual respect.

Talking of respect, let's take a look at some appropriate and acceptable forms of communication with your friends, family and loved ones...

Let me first issue a quick warning: it is NEVER acceptable to physically, mentally, emotionally or sexually harm romantic partners, friends or family. If this is happening to you, please seek professional help.

Appropriate Assertive Family Communication

It's not always easy to know when and how to be assertive with family, friends or romantic partners. The last thing you want is for your attempt at assertiveness to become aggressive or to be taken as such. I've said it numerous times already but it's worth stressing again: respect is at the heart of assertive communication. Stay respectful, no matter what the issue, and you should be able to walk the right line between assertive and aggressive communication. At the same time, being passive with the people you love the most isn't the best means of ensuring the happiness of either side either, is it? One of you will always be being taken advantage of!

The following tips should ensure you approach those nearest and dearest to you with respect and assertiveness:

- Be sure of what your need is and know what you want to communicate before starting the conversation.
- Speak in a calm voice.
- Deliver what you need to say succinctly and with conviction.
- Make your request straightforward and offer concrete examples. For instance, if you want your partner to show you more consideration, ask that he call you if he will be more than [insert your own timescale here] late from work.
- If appropriate, use humor to keep the tone positive and lighthearted. Always use positive language and avoid words that convey blame. Using 'I' statements will help here. *Read to the end of this chapter for more on 'I' statements.*
- If you are in the middle of an emotionally charged situation, in as a level tone as possible, ask for a breather.

This will allow you both to try to address the issue when you have taken a moment and are calmer.
- Always be honest and direct, avoid manipulation, whining or blaming.
- If, in contrast, you find yourself doing any of the following, your communication is NOT appropriate: issuing threats, abusive behavior, mean humor, physical violence, wounding words, and double talk.

So now you know the sort of communication to aspire to with your nearest and dearest but you may be wondering how to achieve it. Given the emotional undercurrents that often swirl around in families and close relationships, it can be a tricky task. The following tips may give you some further help in setting an appropriate and assertive tone in these situations.

Note that the following tips are not written in stone. You may be part of a family that uses strong language, loud voices, and expressive gestures to communicate with one another. Or who issue brutally honest critiques of each other at the drop of a hat. If that is normal for you, and you're happy that it works for everyone, go for it.

If you need a little help, however, you may want to consider the following tips:

- **Keep your emotions in check** – Yes, this one is hard, I know. Conflict by nature breeds emotional distress; you may feel angry, frustrated, attacked or upset. Distressing feelings are perfectly normal but they're not going to help you resolve the problem. If emotions are high, wait before trying to address the issue. Focus on breathing slowly to try to remain calm.
If the other person goads you, try to ignore stepping into the trap and steer the conversation back to the original

292

point. As much as you can, try not to take their criticism or lashing out to heart. If it gets too much, saying you'll address the subject again at a later time/date is a perfectly assertive way of dealing with this.

- **Don't dismiss other people's point of view** – You're working to become assertive and not aggressive, so that means you are not dismissive of other people's points of view. Remember all views are equally valid, even if you don't agree with them. Try to demonstrate your respect and listen to another's point without interruption.

- **Work on developing your empathy** – Following on from above, developing empathy – recognizing and appreciating how the other party views the situation – is probably one of the strongest conflict resolution skills there is. Take their view into consideration and then detail what you need from them. For instance: "I understand that you want to have fun with me and go to the party but it's important for me to complete this work before we go. Can we come up with a plan together that allows us to do both?"

- **Use the technique of negative assertion** – During conflict, people may throw critiques of your personality or behavior in your face. This may be especially true of family members as a family doesn't always hold back. While it's natural to react defensively, this doesn't tend to help anyone. If the comments are true, accept them but don't apologize. However, you can agree with the negative point made, saying something like, "Yes, you make a good point. I don't always listen to everything you have to say." This sort of acceptance tends to take the sting out of your critics' hostility.

- **Adopt a workable compromise** – What happens when you believe your self-respect is in question, yet you haven't done anything wrong? How should you respond then? You could consider a workable compromise with the other party. This doesn't mean that you back down when it's a matter of self-respect or self-worth but that you instead offer a solution that works for both of you. Perhaps something like "I understand that you need to talk to me but I need to finish this first. Shall we meet in one hour and discuss it further?"

At the heart of all the above are two key principles:

**Honesty
&
R–E–S–P–E–C–T**
(Thank you, Aretha, for the soundtrack)

If you work hard to maintain both of these – whether it's during an argument with your partner, a disagreement with a friend, or brutal honesty from your mother – you can't go too far wrong.

Adopting Assertiveness In Difficult Everyday Situations

The above can be used to deal with the little (and large) issues that crop up in day-to-day life with friends, family and partners. But what about those typically awkward situations that even the most confident of us can struggle with from time to time? I'm talking about giving or receiving criticism, dealing with someone manipulative, receiving compliments (blush!) or making complaints. If only there were assertiveness techniques to handle those!

Oh, wait a minute! There are!

Here I want to share some effective techniques to use when faced with some typically awkward scenarios:

When Someone Is Demanding Or Manipulative

- **Use fogging** – Particularly useful if people are behaving in an aggressive or manipulative way towards you. This technique essentially aims for a minimal and calm response but without agreeing to any demands.

   Fogging involves agreeing to any truth in any statements aimed at you, even if critical. By reacting in such an unexpected way, rather than being defensive or argumentative, you effectively take the wind out of the other person's sails, and the confrontation should stop. In essence, you act like a 'wall of fog' – arguments can be thrown out at you but they do not return, instead, disappearing into a 'wall of fog'.

   When things are calmer, you can then discuss the issues more reasonably.

   For example, if someone shouts at you, *"What time do you call this? You said you'd be home an hour ago. I'm fed up with you being late and letting me down all the time."*

   Fogging response: *"I'm later than I wanted to be, I can see it's annoyed you."*

   Shouter: *"Of course, I'm annoyed. You left me waiting for ages."*

   Fogging response: *"Yes, I was concerned you'd be waiting for me."*

And so, on and so forth, until the other party calms down and you can have a reasonable discussion. Fogging allows you, therefore, to receive criticism without getting defensive, and without rewarding manipulation from the other person.

Let's recap…
Fogging involves:

- Acknowledging the criticism.
- Agreeing there may be some truth in the criticism.
- Remaining calm, not getting defensive.
- Remaining the judge of your own actions.

When Receiving Criticism

- **Use negative inquiry** – Many of us naturally get defensive when faced with criticism from our nearest and dearest. Of course, we do – it hurts. When such criticism happens at work, we're more likely to think of it as constructive or attempt to learn from it. But when it's the people closest to us dishing out the feedback, it becomes harder to take. Especially because our friends and relatives may not always temper their words.

  Rather than lashing out, here are a few tips to help you acknowledge the criticism without ruining your relationships:

- First, try to ascertain if it is a genuine criticism or whether there's another reason for the person to be lashing out. Is it because they are angry, sad or frustrated, and you just happen to be there at that moment?

- Keep an open mind. Facing criticism, while hard, can be a chance to learn something about yourself that you didn't know and improve upon it.
- If you believe it to be genuine, acknowledge the criticism. You can first do this by repeating or reflecting it, such as *'So you believe that I...'* and then try to acknowledge any truthful aspects of the criticism, even if it is upsetting to hear.
- Keep in mind that while such truthful criticism tends to wound, it may well be offered in good faith and with the hope that it can be used constructively. It may well be that the person giving the feedback isn't adept at doing so. Try to consider it as a mechanism for self-improvement.

As the name implies, negative inquiry is a way that can help you respond to negative exchanges, such as receiving criticism. Simply put, it's a way of finding out further information and it allows a calm response rather than an angry reaction.

As an example, imagine if someone said about a meal you cooked: *"I couldn't eat it, it was awful."*

Your instinctive reaction might be to say something like, *"How dare you?! I put a lot of effort into making that!"*

But using negative inquiry, you would instead say something like, *"Maybe it wasn't my best, but why couldn't you eat it? What was so bad about it?"*

The theory behind negative inquiry is that it should prompt honest responses, even if negative, to improve overall communication. And possibly even your cooking!

Real Life Case Study – Martine

"My husband and I had a blazing row one day when he told me I favored our natural children over my step-child, his daughter from a previous marriage, says Martine, 43. *"I was floored when he made the accusation. I really didn't believe I did that. I felt that I'd always gone out of my way to include her in our lives, even though she lived with her mother.*

"His criticism felt unfair and wounded me greatly, and my first reaction was to argue back but I stopped myself. I could see that no matter what was said, emotions were too high on either side and we'd never be able to agree or discuss it constructively.

"So, I said I needed to mull over what he'd said, and we tabled the conversation. That night, I tried to rack my brains over his accusation and objectively think of times when I favored our children over his daughter.

"Aside from times when her mother hadn't wanted her to join us, or already had plans, I had included his daughter in everything. The recent time we all went away for the weekend, the swim meets, our other daughter's recital... we always made sure she was invited and, for the most part, she came. She loved her brothers and sister. I also felt like I had a great relationship with her too, so it really hurt me to hear my husband accuse me of something I didn't believe was true."

After 24 hours, Martine approached the conversation again, when both could discuss it more objectively. *"I didn't know what I was doing was called negative inquiry – I only learned that afterward – but I went to my husband, asked if we could discuss his claims from the night before, and I*

298

told him that I'd been racking my brains and couldn't actually think of a time when I acted in the way he alleged. I told him I didn't agree to his generalized claim and asked him if he was thinking of something specific?"

Martine's husband Joe, who had also had time to calm down, felt bad about the argument too but still felt something needed to be said. He struggled to put it into words, however, until Martine asked him for a specific example.

"That's when Joe told me that I didn't discipline his daughter. He said that I put my foot down if any of our shared children were naughty or acting out but I never did it with his daughter. He gave me three specific instances recently where this had happened and explained that he felt it meant I acted as a parent to our three children but not to his daughter."

Martine held her hands up. *"Do you know what? He was right! Each example he gave me was true; I had avoided disciplining his daughter but it wasn't for the reasons he thought. It brought up some issues I'd never discussed with my husband properly, such as the fact that I have never fully known what my role is with his daughter. She has a mother already; in fact, she has two parents who love her and see her regularly. Where did I fit in?*

"I'd decided a while ago that I would simply love her and be there for her but leave the actual 'parenting' to her parents so that I wouldn't step on any toes. I had no idea that my husband expected me to do more, just as he had no idea how unsure of my role I was."

Martine adds: *"I'm so glad now that I didn't just get defensive and dismiss it out of hand. Asking for more information really helped to open up the communication between myself and my husband and brought us closer together."*

Let's recap…
Negative inquiry involves:

- Hearing a critical comment.
- Clarifying that you fully understand the criticism by asking for more information.
- Deciding if the remark is helpful feedback, or
- Choosing to ignore it if it is manipulative.

When Receiving Praise or Compliments

- **Use positive enquiry** – It may be hard to believe for some of us but many people struggle to accept compliments or praise, especially people with low self-esteem. They get embarrassed and tend to either shrug off the compliment or feel the need to return them.

    Have you ever been stuck in that loop? It can get awkward, can't it? Someone says you look nice at a function, for instance, and you feel driven to return the praise and 'panic compliment' them in return. The returned compliment always sounds weak and a little forced, as though you struggled to find something positive to say in return, even when that's not the case.

    Rejecting the compliment or shrugging it off doesn't fare much better either –
    "Lovely dress"
    "What, this old thing?"
    – and only serves to make the giver feel embarrassed and

spurned, and they'll probably never want to give a compliment again.

I once worked with a woman, let's call her Liz, who had terrible self-esteem. For no reason that other people could ever see, she didn't value herself or her work, yet she had a wonderful heart and would do anything for anyone.

Most of us appreciated her for this but it was a struggle to encourage her to see herself through our eyes. She never contacted us outside of work because she didn't believe we'd want to see her. Likewise, she never assumed she was invited to our group work lunches because she didn't really believe people liked her. She was very wrong.

We valued her and it took a lot for us to convince her of that fact. We nearly gave up. Every single compliment or praise was shrugged off or batted away. We'd praise her for something only for her to tell us that she was terrible at something else. She was, to be blunt, hard work. Many people simply stopped trying to befriend her.

I didn't know quite as much about assertiveness then as I do now but even back then I could see that she needed help. So I and another mutual friend persevered and finally became good friends with Liz.

Slowly Liz became more self-confident, started to speak up and gained more confidence in her abilities. I'd love to say that she became super self-confident and assertive but it was – and still is – a slow road. I'm convinced she will get there over time though. I consider Liz a success story for herself but I mention her to demonstrate how your instinctive need to turn down praise and compliments may push people away. It nearly did with Liz and if it had I would have lost out on a really good friend. And Liz would have lost out on numerous important moments in her life.

The truth is that learning to both give and receive compliments GRACEFULLY is an important life skill that helps to signal approval, demonstrate support and boost the other person's self-confidence. Assertive people know how to receive a compliment gracefully, whether or not they agree with it.

Useful phrases to do so include something like:

- *"Thank you, that's so kind of you to say."*
- *"Thank you, it wasn't a problem but I do appreciate you saying so."*

You can also use Positive Enquiry to help you handle praise or positive comments if you struggle with it. Like negative inquiry, this involves asking for more information but doing it during positive feedback rather than negative.

Let's look at an example…

You're holding a dinner party, and someone says, *"Oh you have a lovely house. I love your decorating style."*

Now you could just passively say, *"I didn't do much to it,"* leaving the person complimenting you to feel a bit ashamed that they've been so enthusiastic about it when you obviously aren't.

Or you could use positive inquiry and say, *"Oh, thank you. Do you like any bit in particular?"* Not only does this allow you to find out more and continue the discussion but it gives you the freedom to accept the compliment without getting embarrassed.

A few tips for giving a compliment:

- Make sure your compliment is genuine. People can detect insincerity.
- Realize that compliments work much better than criticism and will be remembered for longer.
- If a compliment isn't appropriate, look for some other way to praise or to say thank you instead.

When Making A Complaint

- **Use the stuck record technique** – When I first started talking about assertiveness and how anyone could learn to become assertive, I had all sorts of people asking me for help. Some wanted to learn how to become self-confident or more confident with the opposite sex, others wanted help to progress at work, and others still just wanted to be able to tackle the daily things that many people take for granted but can be torturous for people with little self-esteem.

  Such as taking something faulty back to the store. That can be a bit challenging for even the most confident of people sometimes, can't it?
  So, here's a great assertiveness technique – called the stuck record technique – for when you need to return something to the store. It's particularly useful if the store staff doesn't want to give you the refund you deserve. It's a way to protect yourself and to demonstrate calm persistence.

  When using this technique, you repeat what you want, as many times as is needed, without getting angry, irritated, frustrated or raising your voice.

  Say the heel broke off your new shoes…

You: *"I bought these shoes new just 10 days ago and the heel fell off yesterday. I want to return them and get a refund please."*

Store assistant: *"These shoes look worn out. Have you worn them every day since? They're only meant for occasional wear."*

You: *"I've only had them for 10 days and the heel fell off. They are faulty and I'd like a refund, please."*

Store assistant: *"We can't give you a refund if you've worn the shoes into the ground."*

You: *"I've only worn them for 10 days and the heel fell off, I would like a refund please."*

And so on and so forth for as long as you need to repeat it until the store assistant finally gets the message and gives in. (And yes, I know, this was a very awkward sales assistant but hey it happens!)

This broken record assertiveness technique allows you to ignore manipulation, baiting and irrelevant logic and stick to the point. By doing so, it takes the sting out of the confrontation and you'll find there's no need to hype yourself up to face similar situations in the future, though you can prepare your message ahead of time if you prefer.

This technique can work in all sorts of situations and not just making complaints (i.e., when someone wants you to do something you don't want to agree to). And while it's a great tool to prevent exploitation, be careful not to use it to bully someone.

Let's recap…

The stuck record technique involves:

- Repeating a request over and over again.
- Staying calm, sticking to the point, not giving up.
- Only accepting a compromise if you are genuinely happy with the outcome. For instance, if our broken shoe-toting woman above was offered another pair of the same shoes instead of a refund, she would have to decide if she was happy with that. If not, she should continue to repeat her request for a refund.

The Importance of 'I' Statements

I touched on *'I'* statements when I talked about the assertiveness LADDER but it's a point worth making again. When discussing any sensitive issues with loved ones or family, using 'I' statements can prevent the blame game and a lot of painful communication.

'I' statements allow you to convey your thoughts or feelings without making accusations. Consider the difference between 'You're wrong' and "I disagree' – don't they seem miles apart? Guess which one would get your partner's back-up when used in a conversation?

Ideally 'I' statements should come with confident body language too, such as direct eye contact, even tone of voice, relaxed posture, as opposed to a passive or aggressive stance.

We know that being assertive helps to strengthen relationships and deepen trust and equality between loved ones, but it's not always easy.

If you're new to 'I' statements, here's a good sentence

structure to use. Assuming you're complaining about someone's behavior, you can start:

'When you -------, I feel ------- because ------. I imagine you probably feel ------ but in the future, I would like us to ------ -.'

Let's put it to the test inserting the action that you're complaining about, how you feel about it and why (your interpretation of the action). Acknowledge their side and perspective, and then offer a suggestion that works for both of you.

Such as...

'When you [come home late], I feel [upset] because [I wanted us to enjoy a meal together and when we don't, I feel distanced from you]. I imagine you probably feel [hemmed in by that], but in the future, I would like us to [eat together at least twice a week so that we can talk more]. How do you feel about that?

You should then listen to their response, ask for clarification if you need it but let them know that you have heard them.

Let's recap...

When using 'I' statements, you should:

- Avoid 'you', 'you always' and similar aggressive blame words or phrases
- Stick with assertive language such as 'I think' and 'I feel'
- Include three elements in all 'I' statements – the behavior you're complaining about, the feeling it gives you, and the consequence to you (tangible effect on you).

All of the above techniques will allow you to communicate openly and honestly but with assertiveness and not aggression. After all, these are your nearest and dearest – strong communication between you is vital.

Chapter 11 – Strong Communication for Strong Women...

Begins With Active Listening!
Entire books have been written on communication in their own right, in far more detail than I can fit into this one, so I'm just going to talk briefly right now about one aspect of assertive communication that you really need to nail. You could say it's the foundation of communicating assertively, and that's **Active Listening**.

I know, I know, you probably think you're a good listener but are you really? The truth is that most of us – women as well as men – don't listen as well as we could. This is especially true during moments of conflict when we're so often concerned with getting our own point across that we don't really listen to the opposing point of view. We're too busy thinking of how to respond, running through scenarios in our heads or getting ready to disagree.

American Educator Edgar Dale's still influential Cone of Experience, which examines learning processes, theorizes that we only remember 25-50% of what we hear. That means that people only really pay attention to half of what you say, at most. Likewise, it also means you are only taking in a quarter to half of what other people say. It's shocking when you think of it like that, isn't it? Think about all that important information are we missing out on?

Listening correctly can impact and improve your professional life, your success and your relationships. It can improve your productivity, as well as your ability to negotiate, influence and persuade other people. It can also help you to avoid misunderstandings and conflict. All of these are crucial for workplace success, and I'd argue, pretty useful for your home life too.
So, how can we listen actively? There are two key parts to active listening:

Tuning In… To What IS And IS NOT Being Said
This is where you make a conscious effort to understand the complete message being communicated, with the verbal side of it being just one small aspect. Whether we're aware of it or not, we listen and interpret what other people tell us via several different sensory modalities. These include sight, sound/tone, touch, proximity, gesture, facial expression, posture, to name just a few. So, in essence, this means paying attention to things like body language, tone of voice, facial expressions whilst looking for any inconsistencies between these and the actual words someone uses. Imagine someone saying they are "fine" but rolling their eyes at the same time – a bit of a giveaway that maybe they're not really fine after all.

Demonstrating Interest
Tuning in is one aspect of active listening but in order for the speaker to feel heard, you also need to demonstrate that you are paying close attention. You can show that you are actually tuned in on all levels through the use of both your verbal and body language. Verbally, you could say something like *'Ah, yes, ok, tell me more,'* etc. While non-verbally you could nod your head, make and maintain eye contact and keep an interested expression on your face.

Think back to a time when you wondered if someone was really listening to you; if you're faced with no reaction at all, you start to feel as if you're talking to a brick wall, don't you? That's a feeling you don't want other people to have while talking with you. So, demonstrate that you are listening and try to do so in a way that encourages him or her to continue speaking. While nodding your head and issuing 'uh-huhs' will help, recapping or asking questions occasionally will communicate that you are listening and correctly understanding the message they are trying to communicate to you.

Taking the time to actively listen to someone shows respect for others and helps to prevent miscommunications and misunderstandings. The good news is that, just like confidence and assertiveness itself, active listening is a skill that can be learned and built upon. Old habits may be hard to break but it can be done, and it starts with the self-awareness to realize where you are falling down.

Bad Listening Habits
Bad listening habits include listening only when it suits you (selective hearing); interrupting, and pseudo-listening (listening while carrying out other tasks, giving your partner or speaker only part of your attention). Ditto, listening without hearing because you're secretly rehearsing what you're going to say next, or disclosing too much information too soon. Not only can this overwhelm the speaker but it's really an indication that you want to respond before hearing the entire message.

Take a moment now to evaluate the last conversation you had. Did you do any of the above?

Be honest.

I have an innate tendency to pseudo-listen and think I can carry on a conversation while simultaneously cooking, cleaning, watching TV, sorting out the kids, etc. As women, we pride ourselves on our multitasking abilities and yet doing too much doesn't always mean you're doing it better. Often, you're simply doing two or three things worse than you would be if you did them one after the other. Listening is one of those things. It's something I still have to work on and practice even now.

Take the time now to evaluate your default listening style and make a point of where you have room for improvement.

Tips to Help You Tune In

- Don't allow yourself to become distracted by whatever else is happening around you and avoid the temptation to form counter arguments in your head while the other person is speaking.
- If you're struggling to concentrate on what someone is saying, try repeating their words mentally as they say them; this should help you focus.
- To demonstrate that you are listening, keep your body posture open and interested, smile and use other facial expressions. Provide small verbal comments and reactions.
- Make sure you understand what is being communicated by asking questions, paraphrasing – 'So it sounds like you're saying….' – summarizing the other person's comments periodically.
- Don't interrupt. Interruptions interfere with the full message and frustrate the speaker. Allow him or her to finish each point before asking questions, or interrupting. Hear the entire message before judging or evaluating it.

- Remember that active listening is a form of respect, so be sure to respond appropriately too. Be respectful in your opinions, honest in your response and treat others as you would want to be treated.
- You can demonstrate that you relate and empathize with your partner/speaker's issues by personalizing the discussion and offering personal examples to show you understand the issue. Beware, however: this is not about you but about your attempt to make the speaker feels heard and understood.
- Avoid leading questions (often used so you can give your own opinions) but ask open-ended queries that should encourage more than simple yes and no answers.
- When responding (after the entire message has been heard!), be careful to make sure that your own non-verbal communication matches your spoken message.

Practice really does make perfect in these situations, so make a point of practicing active listening and assertive communication at all times. Remember the key edict with assertive communication: that it should be open, honest and respectful always.

Make sure therefore that it does not violate another person's rights, doesn't cause guilt or anxiety and considers what each party wants and needs.

Active listening is just one facet of strong assertive communication but it's fair to say that it's the one that the rest of your strong, confident communication should be built upon.

Happy listening.

Conclusion – How Assertive Women Can Change The World

The best way that I know how to inspire you to find the confident, assertive woman within you is to tell you about other women who have already walked the road you travel now. Women who have dug deep and stood tall, for causes, for other women, for themselves…

No woman is born *'confident'*; it's a learned skill and if we're lucky, we'll have people along the way – parents, siblings, family members, friends, teachers, co-workers, mentors, significant others – who will help us find the strong, assertive woman within ourselves.

Even if you don't, or if that woman has been shy about being found until now, it's not too late. It's never too late. Especially if you find a cause, or a person, to inspire you.

I've talked a lot in this book about the confidence crisis among women, about the Gender Bias Backlash that still exists in society today. I don't talk about it to dissuade you or to intimidate you, but to prepare you. There's no doubt that even now, there's still a lot of controversial gender politics around. Some might say, slightly more in recent times. If there wasn't such a disparity in power between men and women, the confidence gap wouldn't exist; neither would the Gender Bias Backlash.

Likewise, all companies would recognize the power of strong, high-level female employees and we'd no longer be hitting our heads on the glass ceiling.

Furthermore, because of the gaps in confidence and power, (provocative political statement coming here) prominent

men – such as the likes of a certain slightly orange colored President of the United States – wouldn't dream of using derogatory language to describe women.
Women would stand as an equally recognized and powerful force and because of that he certainly wouldn't be able to get away with it like he currently does.

Women have borne the brunt of misogyny throughout the ages, and it doesn't stop here. But it inspires me to see women fighting back, to watch them say 'enough is enough' and nowadays, to use the internet as a rallying cry to bring women together.

The Power of Language

Taking back our language is a simple step to equality and assertiveness. If you've ever doubted the power of language to paint a picture, take the supposedly innocent words 'bachelor' and 'spinster'... two words for the same state, one for men and one for women.

Except, they're not equal in their connotations, are they?

Bachelor has come to mean a happily single man, a player, a free man living life to the utmost.

Spinster... well, picture a sad, lonely woman in the corner, probably surrounded by cats, all alone because no one wants to marry her.

Hardly fair, is it?

You won't be surprised to know that language is littered with examples of gender bias like this, many of them much more derogatory. Bitch, slut, bossy, nasty, pussy... these are just some of the derogatory words used against women (very rarely men; have you ever heard a man described as bossy? No, he's just a strong leader). There are obviously much stronger words targeted at women but I don't want to offend anyone with that type of language here.

A revealing 1998 study of gender-linked derogatory terms showed some startling trends in contemporary abusive language towards men and women. For instance, male slurs tend not to be as comparable in offensiveness as the slurs aimed at women. Women's insults also veer towards criticisms or references to sexual morals or female sexual body parts, or to animals (cow, pig, chick, bitch, etc....)

In contrast, derogatory terms aimed at men tend to be associated with weakness or femininity (sissy, pussy), or simply by being associated with women (son of a bitch). Even when men's sexual body parts are used as a slur, they tend to take on non-sexual characteristics and are generally much less offensive than similar ones aimed at women.

Using Language to Condition
Why does this matter? Can't we just ignore the derogatory language and move on? Not really, because such critical language serves a wider purpose... to condition women especially, through verbal aggression and insults, into how they should act. Namely, more well-behaved and self-effacing.

"If you want to change how something is perceived, one way to do it is to change the way you refer to it with language," said Sali Tagliamonte, Ph.D., the chair of the Linguistics Department at the University of Toronto. Such a movement has been taking place across America and the

world in recent years.

"Such A Nasty Woman"
Thus, when Donald Trump – aforementioned most powerful man in the world (and *'he who should certainly know better'*) – described his political opponent, Hillary Clinton, as **'such as nasty woman'**, it exploded as a viral meme and became a rallying cry of its own.

Nasty is a subtly gendered word, directed at women who aren't behaving in the way they're expected to – deferential, non-threatening, feminine. So, it's not surprising that strong, confident, assertive women everywhere wanted to take the word back.

Likewise, Trump's infamous *'grab them by the pussy'* comment inspired angry marches and protests too, with the Women's March on Washington one week after he was elected.

Thousands of women walked through the streets wearing bright cat-eared *'pussy power hats'*, inspired by the Pussyhat Project. Helping to reclaim the word, knit, crochet and demonstrate a sense of humor too.

"Nevertheless, She Persisted"
Senate Majority Leader Mitch McConnell silenced Senator Elizabeth Warren as she challenged Jeff Sessions' nomination for Attorney General, using the explanation, *"She was warned. She was given an explanation. Nevertheless, she persisted."*
Nevertheless, she persisted – **how dare she!**

Women across the world quickly adopted the phrase as their own, transforming it into a feminist motto, becoming a strong call for women to continue to stand up in the face of adversity. The Chicago Tribune wrote: *"Mitch McConnell, bless his heart, has coined a new feminist rally cry."*

'Nevertheless, she persisted' was repeated in countless memes and shout outs across the internet, alongside T-shirts and phone cases, associated with heroic inspirational women from Rosa Parks to Beyoncé to Malala Yousafzai. One particular touching meme associated it with evocative pictures of Ruby Bridges coming out of school alongside her bodyguards, with the hashtag **#ShePersisted.**

No More Slut Shaming
These examples follow the famous Slut Walks, women's attempt to take back the derogatory word 'slut'. Inspired by outrage after a Toronto police officer told a crowd of college-age women that if they didn't want to be assaulted, they shouldn't 'dress like sluts'.

Furious, 3,000 marchers rallied to protest blaming assault survivors for rape, and the Slut Walks were born. Co-founders Heather Jarvis and Sonya Barnett wanted to reclaim the word 'slut' from one that attacks women and their sexuality, to one that empowers.

Whether you believe they've achieved that aim or not, it serves to highlight the unfair discrimination and language associated with women.

Bitch, slut, bossy, nasty… The sticks and stone nursery rhyme may be well-meaning but it's wrong. Words do have power. Never think they don't.

Many of these words have been reclaimed, or attempted to

be reclaimed, by the feminist movement to take away the sting and derogatory meaning behind them. And let me be clear: these women, the ones crocheting Pussy hats and protesting while wearing their 'slutty' clothes, the ones creating viral memes on the internet hitting back at men of power, they are just like you and me. Young and old, affluent and struggling, single and married, black and white… when women band together, we really can change the world.

All it needs is for each one of us to be assertive in our own lives. And remember, until it truly kicks in, there's no shame in faking it 'til you make it.

I'll leave you with one final thought, courtesy of the Queen of Reinvention herself, Madonna. In her album, Rebel Heart, Madonna uses the word 'bitch' no less than 44 times. Yes, she has reclaimed it with panache.

For many though, being called a bitch is a negative thing but should it be? Think about what it really means.

Bitch magazine, founded by women, says: " 'Bitch' was hurled at women who speak their minds, who have opinions and don't shy away from expressing them, and who don't sit by and smile uncomfortably if they're bothered or offended."

So, in other words, assertive, confident women. Like you and me.
Hell yes, I say.

Let's all stand up for the inner Bitch within us all.

Printed in Great Britain
by Amazon